Charles Berlitz is one of the world's foremost authorities on 'natural mysteries'. He is the author of many books, including the highly successful *Mysteries from Forgotten Worlds*, *The Mystery of Atlantis* and the international bestseller, *The Bermuda Triangle*. He is the grandson of the man who founded the famous Berlitz language schools and is himself an accomplished linguist with a working knowledge of some thirty languages. An expert scuba diver, he has been able to combine his hobby with archaeological investigation and he has examined at first hand many of the strange ruins of lost civilizations which have been discovered beneath the sea.

In *Without a Trace*, Charles Berlitz investigates a whole series of new and baffling incidents which have taken place in that mysterious section of the Atlantic Ocean known as the Devil's Triangle – incidents brought to light by the world-wide reaction to his first book. These extraordinary phenomena – previously only known to a handful of people – will surely dispel any lingering doubts that the Bermuda Triangle is still the greatest unsolved mystery of our time.

Also by Charles Berlitz

Mysteries from Forgotten Worlds
The Mystery of Atlantis
The Bermuda Triangle

Charles Berlitz

Without a Trace

with the collaboration of J. Manson Valentine

PANTHER
GRANADA PUBLISHING
London Toronto Sydney New York

Published by Granada Publishing Limited
in Panther Books 1978

ISBN 0 586 04550 3

First published in Great Britain by
Souvenir Press Ltd 1977
Copyright © Charles Berlitz 1977

Granada Publishing Limited
Frogmore, St Albans, Herts AL2 2NF
and
3 Upper James Street, London W1R 4BP
1221 Avenue of the Americas, New York, NY 10020, USA
117 York Street, Sydney, NSW 2000, Australia
100 Skyway Avenue, Toronto, Ontario, Canada M9W 3A6
Trio City, Coventry Street, Johannesburg 2001, South Africa
CML Centre, Queen & Wyndham, Auckland 1, New Zealand

Made and printed in Great Britain by
Richard Clay (The Chaucer Press) Ltd
Bungay, Suffolk
Set in Linotype Times

Dedicated to those who, in attempting to solve the mystery of the Bermuda Triangle, have offered their experience, their expertise, their time, equipment, resources – and sometimes their lives.

Contents

Foreword

I am the author of *The Bermuda Triangle*, a book that caused a considerable controversy in 1975–76, and that has attained sales of over 5,000,000 in English and twenty other languages. I am often asked about why the Bermuda Triangle, an area between Florida, the Sargasso Sea, and Bermuda, where ships and planes have been disappearing without trace for half a century or more, has proved to be of such interest to all parts of the country and even the world, where even countries on the other side of the earth have developed a preoccupation with the Bermuda Triangle. Fascination with the Triangle is based upon the mystery, the menace of unknown forces, danger, and presumed death or disappearance into a void – a potent combination.

Since a considerable number of books and countless newspaper and magazine articles have subsequently been published, most of them dealing with the mystery and some explaining that there is no mystery, what, one may ask, is the purpose of another book about the Bermuda Triangle?

The aim of this present book is neither to refute, inform, nor educate critics of the reality of the mystery, but rather to examine previously unrecorded and new incidents as well as current developments within the Triangle. These seem to fit within a larger picture as well as to lead further and deeper into mysteries of ever-broadening scope.

Since *The Bermuda Triangle* was published, I have received thousands of letters from readers in the United States and scores of other countries throughout the world, and telephone calls at various hours of the day and night. Over half of these messages were from people who personally had undergone unusual experiences in the Triangle. Now that my book had brought the matter out into the open, they wanted to communicate their experiences, which had been disbelieved or derided to the point where they themselves had begun to believe that they must have imagined what they saw. Others, who had been on duty with the Navy, Air Force, or commercial airlines, had been warned not to discuss the incidents they had witnessed. At lectures I have given since publication in North America and Europe, almost invariably some ex-member of the services or a merchant marine survivor of incidents will address the audience with an extemporaneous account of an experience that could not be told before.

It was as if a great mine of untapped information had been inadvertently uncovered by the publication of *The Bermuda Triangle*, information that, while suggesting a variety of explanations, seemed to be pointing to a possible solution so unusual as to be almost inconceivable according to our normal concepts.

From the testimony of these many witnesses and survivors it has been possible to ascertain that a considerably greater number of disappearances has taken place than previously calculated, and that many more people, sailing or flying through the area, have undergone experiences which then appeared and still appear inexplicable and even unbelievable but which may fit within a more comprehensive explanation, however incredible the explanation itself may seem.

In addition to these new, or previously unreported experiences, a number of privately funded 'Triangle' expeditions by boat, plane, scuba, or a combination of all three have taken place in the area during 1975–76 with, on several occasions, rather unexpected results.

It is no longer necessary to bring the question of the Bermuda Triangle out into the open; it is already there. It is more pertinent to examine these new developments, not only to reconsider a zone of possible danger and to seek to establish norms of relative safety, but also to explore more deeply the attendant mysteries of our own environment, where familiar areas, although already superficially explored, may not always be what they seem.

CHAPTER ONE

THE DEEPENING MYSTERY

Although prior to the 1970s information about the Bermuda Triangle was tantalizingly nebulous, a number of people had known about it for a long time. These were pilots, civilian and military, crews of naval and civilian ships, fishermen, reporters, researchers, and certain sections of the public in the general area bounded by Bermuda in the north, Florida in the west, and, in the east, a point in the ocean in the vicinity of 40° west longitude. Many of these individuals, especially those involved in sailing or flying over the area, either kept completely or selectively silent about their own experiences in the Triangle. The reason for their secrecy came from either fear of ridicule, loss of credibility, or even from an inclination to believe that it was bad luck to talk about it. In the words of a young man who grew up on the Atlantic coast of Florida and still wishes to be unidentified:

> We used to hear bits of information about the Triangle, but it always seemed to be hushed up. The kids would sometimes hear older people talking about it – weird things – but you would have to pry it out of them. You couldn't just go up to them and say 'What's been happening in the Triangle?'

Reports about this unusual area, where planes and ships, together with their passengers and crews, continued over a period of years (as well as now) to disappear without a trace, generally in good flying and sailing weather conditions, had usually appeared in news items or in the form of brief references in books which did little more than provoke the reader's curiosity.

The elements of information about the Bermuda Triangle are both intriguing and somewhat sinister; in an area of the Western Atlantic in a general triangular shape between Bermuda, Florida, and the 40° meridian, scores of ships and planes have been disappearing in the last thirty years with no indication of what has happened to them, since neither wreckage nor survivors have been found. Ships and planes have been seen by people on other craft to enter a localized and sometimes luminous fog or cloud – and not to emerge. Ships large and small, several with crews of three hundred men, have vanished without explanation. Aircraft, military and commercial, disappear from the sky while preparing to land. British South American Airlines lost three of its planes, complete with passengers, two of them in the Triangle, after having sent normal radio reports, and another after it had passed through the Triangle – and given a final garbled word of alarm. Military and naval planes, flown by experienced pilots in good weather, have disappeared without an SOS or 'Mayday' message. On one notable occasion, in December 1945, a whole flight of Marine bomber aircraft disappeared on a training flight during which time their base, at Fort Lauderdale, Florida, could overhear their intercom conversations although the pilots could not hear the base. Their messages concerned spinning compasses, nonfunctioning gyros and locators, a general bewilderment about where they were, and curious comments about white water and that the sea did not 'look like it should.' A rescue plane sent out to assist them disappeared approximately at the time it entered the search area.

If this is not a mystery, it is certainly a good approximation of one.

The mystery is compounded by the fact that many of these disappearances seem not to be connected with storms or hurricanes, as the great majority of them have taken place in good weather. Moreover, almost all wrecks leave *something* – floating or washed-up wreckage, lifeboats or life rafts, or even an oil slick on the water which, despite the many extensive search and rescue operations, have been notably lacking in the case of the disappearing craft. Messages from some of the aircraft prior to their disappearance have given no indication of trouble; in effect, one minute they are on course and then, without warning, they are gone, almost as if something had snatched them from the sky, or unexpected and gigantic whirlpools had pulled them under the surface of the sea, or an unidentified force had caused their disintegration.

Whatever the reason for the disappearances, the number of them was eminently impressive. Once the curtain of silence was lifted and new as well as formerly unpublicized reports began to come in, it became evident that the figure of a hundred ships and planes and a thousand people lost without a trace in the Triangle was a low estimate and something like double this figure would be more accurate. (In the period 1974–76 more than six hundred yachts and other pleasure craft have disappeared off the coasts of the United States, a considerable percentage of these losses occurring within the Bermuda Triangle.)

Books and articles dealing with the Bermuda Triangle have been generally concerned with detailing the disappearances of craft and people and then 'closing the case' by attributing the losses to easily explained or unknown causes. Since there were never any survivors the circumstances of the disappearances could scarcely be considered in detail and compared with each other. It was not generally realized that many individuals had experienced unusual events on the fringe of an anomaly within the Triangle and had *not* disappeared. They had maintained a discreet silence, keeping their experiences to themselves or their immediate families and associates.

From the very first months of publication of *The Bermuda Triangle* letters and telephone calls by the thousands began coming in to the publishers, to radio stations and television networks who had produced shows relating to the Bermuda Triangle, to the editors of newspapers and magazines that published articles about the book, and to me personally. These were principally from persons who wished to inform someone about their own experiences within the Triangle, an action they had previously hesitated to take because of presumed popular disbelief, fear of ridicule, or of compromising their careers. In some cases they had already made reports to pertinent authorities, but such reports had been ignored, downgraded, or simply 'filed'. These reports from 'survivors,' if they can be so designated, have come from cities and towns throughout the United States, Canada, Great Britain, islands within the Bermuda Triangle, and other parts of the English-speaking world. They come from seamen, boat owners, pilots and passengers, and especially from ex-service United States, Canadian, or British and other British Commonwealth military or navy personnel who have personally witnessed incidents within the Triangle area. Many of them have supplied copies of flight reports or log extracts to validate their information. (In this case emphasis should be put on the prefix 'ex-' as military or naval personnel presently on active duty are understandably reticent to be quoted.) A number of communications as well came from family members of those mysteriously lost, in the hope that the author might have some additional information which they had been unable to obtain from government sources, often implying that information was apparently being withheld for unspecified reasons.

Then, when *The Bermuda Triangle* was translated into twenty languages and I travelled abroad on lecture tours, reports were sent to me from a variety of foreign countries including some from the other side of the Iron Curtain in what might be termed a Bermuda Triangle 'détente.' Reports came from Japan, comparing the Bermuda Triangle with the Devil Sea off its coast and suggesting a possible connection; from Germany, where researchers in astronomy suggest that the Bermuda Triangle is an open window to the cosmos; from Indonesia, where large ships have been found, as in the Bermuda Triangle, inexplicably empty of passengers or crew; from Australia and New Zealand, where time and dimensional anomalies have been noted in the vastnesses of the Pacific; from Argentina and Brazil, where a zone of anomaly exists off their coasts in which unusual craft seem to appear out of the sea and fly into the sky; from Spain, where a leading investigator connects UFO sightings in the Caribbean with other past miracles *and* demoniac manifestations; and from Bermuda itself, where memories of other unpublicized disappearances have been reawakened by public interest in the mystery.

The greater number of these reports are characterized by a common theme of aberrant electromagnetic activity such as the spinning of compasses, malfunction of gyros, radio, radar, and sonar blackout, instrument malfunction, drain of electric power, and malfunction of motors. In addition, reports tell of shining and pulsating lights seen in the night sky or beneath the sea, sudden glowing fogs, sightings of UFOs and USOs (Unidentified Submarine Objects), the inexplicable loss or gain of time on air flights as well as the well-witnessed appearances of 'phantom' ships and planes appearing, disappearing, or crashing (in complete silence), as if repeating an incident lost in time. Many of these reports touch on previously unreported phenomena which, although apparently unrelated, may be relevant to the over-all mystery of the Triangle.

Some of these new reports tell of bright lights at night, moving above and also under the sea, evidently connected with the electronic drain and stoppage of all ship or plane power sources during the period of their proximity. Others deal with loss of boats in tow, while surrounded by a fog which covered only the area in their immediate vicinity. A pilot tells of incredible magnetic storms accompanied by purple lightning flashes lasting more than five seconds, leaving the air strong with the smell of burned ozone.

Some accounts border on the supranatural:

* A Cessna 172 is 'chased' by a cloud, causing its instruments to malfunction, with consequent loss of its position

and the death of its pilot, as reported by surviving passengers.

* A Beechcraft Bonanza flies into a monstrous cumulus cloud off Andros, loses radio contact and then regains it after four minutes, but finds itself now over Miami with twenty-five more gallons of gas than it should have had – almost exactly the amount of gas it *would have burned* for the Andros–Miami trip.

* A National Airlines 727 is lost on radar for ten minutes during which time the pilot reports flying through a light fog. Upon landing it is found that all watches on board and the plane's chronometer have lost exactly ten minutes in spite of a time check half an hour before landing.

* An Eastern Airlines flight suffers a tremendous jolt, a loss of altitude and lands at a nonscheduled stop. Flying and nonflying personnel and passengers find that their watches have stopped at the approximate time of the jolt and the plane's fuselage shows indications of having suffered a fusing blast of intense heat or electricity.

Other reports indicate a sort of time warp or replay of past events:

* A plane is seen in daylight by hundreds of people to crash in shallow water at a well-frequented beach, but no trace of it is found.

* A Cessna 172 is observed by the tower personnel of the airport at Grand Turk Island in the Bahamas, but the tower cannot communicate with the pilot. The tower, however, can hear the pilot tell her passenger that she must be over the wrong island because 'there's nothing down there.' Pilot and passenger then fly off to oblivion.

* A mate on watch on a cargo ship notes his ship turning in a circle, all navigational instruments affected, and a 'ball of fire' almost carries him from the deck while passing low over the ship.

* A crew member on the *Queen Elizabeth 2* sees a plane flying directly at his ship. The plane suddenly disappears into the sea a hundred yards from the ship. The sea

merely opens; there is no splash, no noise, and no wreckage or oil.

* Shipmasters sighting ships enter names in their logs, but the ships that they see have long been listed as sunk or disappeared.

* An enormous 'rising moon' of water arises from the ocean and is observed by personnel of the U.S.S. *Josephus Daniels* – a guided missile destroyer. The ship changes course. The log is examined in port but is never returned to the ship.

These incidents, some quite recent, which will be treated in subsequent chapters, serve to point up the different kinds of anomalies present in the Bermuda Triangle and may furnish, together with the record of the past thirty years, some indication as to what forces are present in the Triangle and what has been happening to the ships, planes, and people.

This enormous backlog of personal experience, even while taking into account possibilities of hallucination or misapprehension, may prove to be an excellent source of information for the eventual solution of a mystery that, in spite of its vociferous detractors, has yet to be explained.

Detractors of the concept of the so-called Bermuda Triangle represent an established adverse opinion especially prevalent in oceanographic, scientific, meteorological, and aeronautical circles. Members of these groups usually take a stand that falls into one or more of the following categories:

1. The Bermuda Triangle furor is simply a sensational plot to capture public interest.
2. The Bermuda Triangle does not exist as a danger area or as any other kind of area.
3. If an area of magnetic aberration does exist, it is not strong enough to cause serious concern.
4. Any unexplained sinking or disappearance can be automatically called a mystery until the cause is discovered.
5. Plane ditchings or explosions in flight may result from many causes; lack of visible evidence being explained by the truism that 'It's a big ocean.'

6. The vanishing ships might have been lost in sudden storms, sunk by underwater seismic activity, been hijacked and repainted, or been 'run over' by larger ships.

Criticism of the concept of the Bermuda Triangle among the above groups is understandable, especially in the case of commercial airlines and maritime transport companies. It is notable, however, as opposed to airline officers who have experience in the area, that some of the most vehement opponents of the presence of an ongoing mystery in the section of the Atlantic covered by the Bermuda Triangle have either not had the opportunity to visit it personally, do not deem it necessary to make an on-the-spot investigation, or have discreetly kept away from it.

As for the oceanographers, geologists, and meteorologists who are familiar with the area, again it is understandable that they would be unwilling to admit the possibility of a mystery in the many disappearances other than the presence of freak storms and uncertain weather conditions. Such ready explanations, however, do not furnish a reason for the absence of wreckage of any kind after a disappearance, which occurs only in this area. There are no survivors, no boats, life rafts, life preservers, wreckage, oil slicks, or even shark packs, which habitually linger in areas where there has been a recent crash or sinking. On the other hand, the very absence of survivors or wreckage could be explained, according to many who believe that unknown forces are at work within the Triangle, by the possibility that the craft and occupants did not necessarily go down into the ocean, but rather *up* into the sky, through a reversal of gravity or by collection by extraterrestrial entities, or even out – into another dimension – through disintegration as a result of encountering an extremely high magnetic field or a field of ionization, the latter perhaps in turn caused by pathways of extraterrestrial spacecraft.

It is these theories that tend to cause members of the scientific or governmental establishment to deny the very existence of the Bermuda Triangle even while planes and ships continue to disappear in what appear to be uncomfortably increasing numbers. It is both easier and safer to deny the actuality of a phenomenon than to attempt to explain the unexplainable – to consider powers or latent forces not yet scientifically 'acceptable,' and to lay oneself open, at the very least, to accusations of sensationalism, cultism, and an overly active imagination.

The U.S. Seventh Coast Guard District, which is responsible for the search and rescue missions for ships and planes lost at sea in this area, is more than aware of the Bermuda Triangle because of the numerous requests for information and assurance from concerned air and sea travelers and boat owners who contemplate flying or sailing through the area. In answer to these requests, too numerous to be treated separately, the Seventh Coast Guard District has composed a form letter which, in its first paragraph, assures the addressee that the 'Bermuda or Devil's Triangle' is an imaginary area, and thereupon proceeds to give its boundaries and to discuss special magnetic characteristics.

While it would scarcely be likely that the Coast Guard would admit an explanation besides human error or climatic variations, it is interesting nonetheless to note certain quotations from Coast Guard Headquarters such as that offered in answer to a question about the Bermuda Triangle:

> ... The Navy is trying to get to the bottom of the mystery with a project ... in which they are investigating electromagnetic gravitation and atmospheric disturbances. Some experts think that some such disturbance might have disintegrated those planes in 1945 ...'

Recently, during a press interview in San Francisco, I was asked by a reporter whether any disappearances had been noted recently. I replied that a plane had vanished the previous week and suggested that the disappearances in the Bermuda Triangle, far from being a footnote to the past history of the sea, are still continuing on the average of a plane about every two weeks and a ship or yacht almost weekly. This was based on the on-the-spot observations of

Dr Manson Valentine and colleagues who are presently engaged in researching the Bermuda Triangle in the waters off Miami, Fort Lauderdale, the Florida coast and Keys, Bermuda, and the Bahamas.

One reporter, on hearing these disquieting figures, phoned the Seventh Coast Guard District to ask them what they thought of this 'sensational' report. He was unprepared for the reply he received. The Coast Guard told him the figures sounded 'not out of bounds.' This, of course, does not mean that the Coast Guard holds that such vanishing people have become the prey of sea monsters, extraterrestrial space-nappers, or are the victims of magnetic disintegration – there are many other, more terrestrial possibilities including mutiny, hijacking, and change of identity – however, the disappearances continue to take place, without traces of passengers or crews.

Retired and active members of the United States Navy seem to be in disagreement about the mystery of events in the Bermuda Triangle. Admiral Samuel Eliot Morison, United States Navy, Retired, after making a somewhat laconic initial observation – 'It's almost all hooey' – went back to questioning Columbus' reported observation of the 'mysterious glowing white waters' in the Bahamas area. However questionable Columbus' report may have been, he not only remarked on the streaks of glowing waters but also reported what we might now label a UFO, described by him as a flying 'bad' (or flickering) candle or torch which left trails of sparks, circled his ship, and plunged into the sea.

A Navy spokesman cited by *Time* magazine has suggested, with moderately successful irony, that a 'Triangle' book could be written about 'The Sable Triangle,' fixed on Sable Island, Nova Scotia, a site of hundreds of shipwrecks. But 'wrecks' is the key word in this boutade, for, unlike other danger areas for ships, such as Cape Hatteras, Cape Horn, the Cape of Good Hope, the Great Australian Bight, and Sable Island itself, it is not the wrecks, of which the Bermuda Triangle has had a full (and identifiable) complement, but the disappearances without trace of ships, planes and large numbers of people, which comprise the element of mystery here.

Not all Navy and, above all, naval aviation personnel are in accord with official Navy pronouncements about the Triangle. A senior intelligence officer of the Third Naval District Headquarters, without, however, authorizing the use of his name, has expressed himself as follows: '... Nobody in the Navy sneers at this thing. We have always known there's something strange about this Bermuda Triangle. But nobody has found out what it is. There doesn't seem to be any physical or logical reason. It's almost as if these ships had been suddenly covered by some sort of electronic camouflage net.' A member of the Board of Inquiry investigating the loss of five TBM Avenger bombers and the Martin Mariner rescue plane sent out after them from Fort Lauderdale Naval Air Base in December 1945 expressed himself more succinctly when he observed: 'We don't know what the hell is going on out there.'

Personnel on flying status are also inclined to be less skeptical about the forces at work in the Bermuda Triangle. A radio phone-in call received by the author during a Miami interview came from a Navy captain who said: 'I'm a Navy captain with thirty thousand hours' flying time in what you call the Bermuda Triangle' – adding after a short silence, 'And I'm glad someone has finally come out and faced what we Navy pilots have known about for many years.'

Commercial airline executives consider the Bermuda Triangle controversy with a certain lack of enthusiasm. Eastern Airlines, which suffered a loss by disintegration of Eastern Flight 401, a Lockheed L-1011, near the Miami Airport in December 1972, has recently published an issue of their inflight magazine featuring an article on 'The Great Bermuda Triangle Rip-off.' The airline's position becomes understandable not only from a commercial viewpoint but also from the bother of answering frequent questions on the part of the passengers who demand, 'When do we go into the Bermuda Triangle?' or 'Do we cross the Bermuda Triangle or fly around it?' Conversely, passengers have occasionally been told by airport information clerks that planes they were expecting had been delayed because 'the pilot wanted to fly around the Triangle.'

Sometimes the pilot himself will beat the passengers to the 'punch line,' as in the case of an Eastern Airlines charter flight en route from Nova Scotia to the Caribbean in March 1975. Flying close to the coast of Florida, the pilot announced over the intercom : 'Passengers sitting on the left side of the plane can now see where the infamous Bermuda Triangle begins. Thank God we are not flying through it!' This sort of approach tends to infuse trips to the Bermuda Triangle with a certain verve, echoed by the Bermudians themselves who have composed a calypso about the Bermuda Triangle, customarily greeted with cheers of recognition when played on the dance floor.

Even a certain amount of Bermuda Triangle black humor has surfaced in the airlines. One story is : Some airline executives are on a flight between Bermuda and Florida and one of them, as a joke, sends the captain a jerkily handwritten message : 'Do you know we are in the Bermuda Triangle?' To which the captain replies : 'Can't worry about that now. All my instruments are off and my compasses are spinning.'

A ship's position within the Triangle is frequently a matter of interest and comment to naval surface and submarine craft operating in its waters. Robert Hayes, of White Plains, New York, formerly a boiler technician on the guided missile heavy cruiser the U.S.S. *Albany* (CG-10), remembers that the subject was discussed with considerable interest by the crew as they headed through the Triangle to Mayport, Florida :

We knew when we were entering the Triangle because some of the people who were working on radar had told other crew members. We had a big map – 6 or 7 feet across – on the bulletin board which charted the ship's position. Someone drew a triangle on the map, so the whole ship knew about it and talked about it. Everyone seemed to be talking about it and wondering what was out there. One of the Firsts said: 'It's some kind of time warp – it's out there alright, but you can't see it.' Another First said: 'Well, I hope we are not going to be another statistic.'

Whether or not the Bermuda Triangle is an area in which mysterious forces are present as a danger to ships, planes, and people, it is certainly an area of magnetic aberration and is so indicated on air and sea charts including those of the British Admiralty. It is generally known by all who fly or sail over the area that frequently the compass needles spin, the gyros malfunction, radio communication tends to become sporadically interrupted, and unidentified lights and impressive magnetic storms are a matter of frequent occurrence. However, any attempt to link these phenomena with the well-authenticated disappearances of the many ships, planes, and people in the area is, for public consumption at least, denied or ridiculed by the authorities and subjected to considerable derision in the press, first in the United States and then, as the reputation of the Bermuda Triangle spreads, throughout the world. The following headlines are indicative of the somewhat sportive attitude of the press as well as an understandable oversimplification of some of the possible explanations: 'ARE THERE HIJACKERS IN OUTER SPACE'; 'LOST ATLANTIS IS ALIVE AND WELL AND COLLECTING PLANES AND SHIPS.' British newspapers feature: 'HOW THE QE II ALMOST ENDED UP IN A SPACE MUSEUM'; Dublin newspaper headlines: 'YOUR FRIENDS MAY BE IN A MARTIAN ZOO'; French magazines rhetorically ask: 'WHAT IS IT THAT DISINTEGRATES PLANES AND SHIPS IN THE BERMUDA TRIANGLE?' German press editorials discuss: 'LASER BEAMS FROM THE SEA BOTTOM' and 'IS THERE A HOLE IN THE SKY?'

Oceanographers and meteorologists generally ascribe the alleged disappearances to sudden weather changes and explain the lack of wreckage and oil slicks as being due to the flow of the Gulf Stream, which flows north between Florida and the Bahamas at a rate of 1.5 to about 4 knots. Accord-

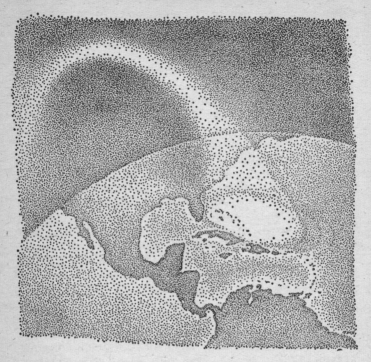

1. Certain theories relating to the Bermuda Triangle suggest that it is a space probe or point of entry facilitated by natural forces for visitors employing theoretical curvature of space and time.

ing to this theory, the wreckage of a plane or ship would drift north of its point of initial disappearance and therefore be unlocatable at or near its last reported position. But since the rate of the Gulf Stream is no mystery, it seems logical that it would occur to search and rescue units of the Coast Guard to look in the calculated area of drift as well as the last reported location, and in general this is standard procedure. It is of further interest to point out that meteorologists customarily plot out developing weather and storms in a fan-shaped area called the 'Devil's Triangle,' which, for the meteorologists at least, certainly exists as a place if not as a phenomenon.

A further contribution to the deepening mystery of the Bermuda Triangle has come from an unexpected source – the weather satellites. Professor Wayne Meshejian, a physicist at Longwood College, Virginia, who with his assistants has been plotting satellite pictures for over three years, has observed that, for the last two years, the NOAA (National Oceanographic and Atmosphere Administration) polar orbited satellites at an altitude of eight hundred miles have frequently begun to malfunction *only* while over the Bermuda Triangle. Of the two pictures taken by the satellites, clear and taped, the taped signal often ceases transmission when the satellite enters the Bermuda Triangle area, and telemetric and electronic pulses from the satellite are also wiped out. In attributing this, as he does, to 'some kind of external energy source under the water' or to an enormous magnetic field in the area that is erasing the magnetic tape on which the visible pictures are stored, it is interesting to note that, while the magnetic field is strong enough to erase a tape eight hundred miles above the earth, it does not interfere with the orbit pattern of the satellite. But a magnetic field strong enough to erase the tape would in Meshejian's words, 'definitely affect the ease with which the satellite goes through space ... with a field this strong it should be able to make the satellite swerve out of orbit, but this is not happening, so we are talking about a force we don't know anything about.' While Meshejian lays himself open to allegations of sensationalism from the governmental-scientific establishment, the latter, nevertheless, still has no answer to a pertinent question Meshejian poses: 'Why only over this part of the earth?'

While compass and instrument aberrations have been noted on surface ships, low-flying and high-altitude planes, the possibility that the eight-hundred-mile-high satellites could also be affected causes one to wonder how far up – or out – the field (or pathway?) of aberration may extend.

Professor Meshejian was later contacted by the pertinent government agency, and it was suggested to him that it would be helpful if he disclaimed his report, as it had elicited numerous inquiries as well as suggestions that information was being withheld. An official explanation finally offered to Meshejian held that the 'blackout' was due to rewinding although, if this were so, the automatic rewind operation would be a surprisingly inefficient one, varying from half a minute to several hours. It is further noteworthy that this explanation was offered a full six months *after* publication of the Meshejian findings. As for Professor Meshejian, he is still of the opinion that 'it is possible that there is a magnetic field doing it.'

As might have been expected, Professor Meshejian's independent observations met with a notable lack of enthusiasm on the part of government officials. A spokesman for the National Environmental Satellites Service, in offering his assurance, followed the technique of coupling the theory under consideration with a more fantastic one in order better to scotch it: 'I guarantee it's nothing in the Bermuda Triangle any more than there's a hole in the North Pole,' adding pointedly, 'as some people think.'

Every time the question of incidents and disappearances within the Triangle comes before the public, an apparent reflex reaction among official spokesmen impels them vigorously to deny that there exists anything unusual in, above, or below the waters of the Bermuda Triangle.

But notwithstanding these constant denials from assorted authorities and experts in oceanography, aeronautics, meteorology, and other fields, ships, planes, and people continue to disappear. In addition reports (that probably would not have been made previously) from pilots, ship captains, crews, boat owners, and passengers who have observed unusual occurrences in the Triangle are now being submitted in greater quantity and provide a base for correlation and comparison.

But even if all the disappearances of ships, planes, and

people were the result of pure coincidence, it is still evident, based on the increasing number of reported incidents, that there exist within the Triangle unusual magnetic, weather, and perhaps gravitational anomalies and that they have affected and are still affecting ships, planes – and their occupants.

The fact that the majority of incidents have taken place within a certain area would suggest that there could be something on the sea bottom itself, perhaps man-made and left over from another time, that was causing the unusual magnetic forces. But the extent of the aberrations and disappearances, and their varying intensity at different times and places, indicates a moving phenomenon of some sort, natural or perhaps controlled. An examination of the now considerably revised number of the disappearing ships and planes, the times and places that they vanished, their cargoes, and their last messages, if any, should provide – if not an explanation – at least a convenient tally sheet of these voyages to oblivion.

CHAPTER TWO

VOYAGES TO OBLIVION: A ROLL CALL

The Bermuda Triangle has been an area of danger, mystery, and often doom ever since the early European discovery of the West Indies. From the very first navigational reports of the early Spanish sea captains, starting with Columbus, it has been evident that unusual electromagnetic or other forces are present in the Bermuda Triangle, especially in its western area. Columbus' very first voyage, before landfall, experienced a sort of preview of the unusual; first a view of the 'glowing waters' of the Bahamas and then what appeared to be a fireball which circled his flagship and then plunged beneath the sea. At the same time his crew, notoriously on the edge of mutiny, felt their doubts on the necessity of the voyage increase when they noted the erratic behavior of the ship's compass, which began to turn in complete circles to the consternation of the pilots.

Some of Columbus' further experiences within the then unnamed Bermuda Triangle might be said to have anticipated the more striking examples of phenomena that have given the area its sinister reputation. In September 1494 he observed a sea monster off Hispaniola (Haiti–Santo Domingo) which he, in the custom of his time, interpreted as a storm warning and secured his ships. In June 1494 an unusual 'whirlwind' sank three of his ships by: 'turning them three or four times about ... without any storm or roughness of the sea.' In May 1502, Columbus, on another expedition, and foreseeing a storm (we have no record whether he had been warned by another sea monster) asked the Governor of Hispaniola for permission to anchor his four ships in the harbor of Santo Domingo and, at the same time, warned Governor Boabdilla not to give the order for the departure of a treasure fleet of thirty galleons to Spain. The governor ignored the advice and subsequently lost twenty-six of the treasure ships in a sudden violent tempest which seemed to witnesses to exhibit the characteristics of a naval battle – 'a sustained bombardment leaving the smell of burnt powder in the air.' Fortunately (or unfortunately) for Columbus, the one ship that got through to Spain carried Columbus' personal treasure, a coincidence that certainly did not aid his position at court. Six months later a treasure fleet of seventeen vessels also vanished in a sudden tempest equally marked by what we would now recognize as extraordinary electromagnetic manifestations.

Columbus doubtlessly through his superior seamanship avoided becoming a victim of the unusual storms in the area. In one case, in December 1502, when a giant waterspout formed between two of his ships, Columbus had his sailors recite the Gospel according to St John and continue until the waterspout dissolved. But with all his good fortune in navigation, Columbus was destined to founder on the shoals of the dislike of an envious and jealous monarch, who suspected him of maladministration, pride, overambition, and perhaps too much wisdom. One might even ascribe the unfortunate end of the great discoverer's career (his death in prison) as one of the first historic tragedies connected with the Bermuda Triangle.

But the Spanish treasure ships which were wrecked by sudden storms and subsequent pirate or privateer forays on Spanish galleons throughout the centuries have left wrecks on island beaches and the coasts of the Spanish colonial lands which included Florida and also north through Georgia and the Carolinas. Due to lack of effective communication in early days it cannot be judged whether ships 'disappeared' in the Bermuda Triangle from reasons other than the activities of pirates or sudden storms. Legends of the sea, however, did soon come into existence, concerning early disappearances of galleons and warships from other, more mysterious causes, coupled with reports of occasional sightings of these 'lost ships' aimlessly adrift, generally in the Sargasso Sea, which forms the eastern part of the Triangle.

The northern extremity of the alleged Triangle, Bermuda itself, discovered in 1515, soon acquired a somewhat sinister reputation for the unexplained disappearance of certain ships. One of the earliest Bermudian references to disappearing boats concerns a longboat sent out by survivors from the wreck of the *Sea Venture*, which foundered off Bermuda in 1609 while on its way to the new American colonies. The longboat with its seven crew members vanished at sea and was seen no more by the anxious survivors, who finally built a new craft to escape from Bermuda, which they described as 'terrible to all that touched upon it' – an opinion considerably at odds with our present concept of this pleasant island.

Shakespeare, writing his plays during this period, must have heard something of Bermuda's reputation directly or indirectly from seafarers of the time, as he has immortalized an early allusion to the area in *The Tempest* (Act 1, Scene II) when Ariel says:

> '... where once
> Thou call'dst me up at midnight to fetch dew
> From the still vexed Bermoothes, there she's hid ...'

From accounts of the days of sailing ships, the 'Bermudas' and areas to the south were indeed 'vexed' for hundreds of years by disappearances of vessels whose fates formed part of the larger pattern of ships lost in the ocean, and whose disappearances were usually ascribed to tempests, piracy, or mutiny. Only in the nineteenth and especially the twentieth centuries did improved communications and ships' records indicate that there was something peculiarly disquieting about the many losses in the area, especially the absence of any survivors, wreckage, or, after radio communication came into general use, any indication as to what was happening or had happened to the disappearing vessels. Moreover, a considerable number of these mysterious disappearances concerned only the passengers and crews – otherwise the abandoned vessels seemed to be shipshape, with logs, lifeboats, cargoes, and even personal effects in place.

These events, intriguing as they were, would probably have continued to contribute to the legendary mysteries of the sea, especially of the Sargasso Sea, a great part of which is included within the confines of the Bermuda Triangle, if it were not for the dawning realization that planes were encountering unusual experiences and were also disappearing in considerable numbers in the same area as the vanishing ships. Pilots had long been aware of plane disappearances within the area, sometime before and during World War II, but had attributed them to normal incidents of plane accidents or to war conditions and possible enemy action. They had also noted certain unusual occurrences that marked their flights through the Triangle area. Charles Lindbergh himself may have been one of the very first pilots to make a note of the curious compass and instrument abnormality over the area. On a flight in *The Spirit of St Louis* from Havana to the mainland on February 13, 1928, he entered in his log:

Both compasses malfunctioned over Florida Straight, at night. The earth indicator needle wobbled back and forth. The liquid compass card rotated without stopping. Could recognize no stars through heavy haze. Located position, at daybreak, over Bahama Islands, nearly 300 miles off course. Liquid compass card kept rotating until the Spirit of St Louis reached the Florida Coast.

Lindbergh, at this time, was involved in an early development of passenger routes for Pan American Airlines. These were the days when planes had only electromagnetic compasses to find magnetic north, direction finders that could vary from other strong magnetic influences. Several months later in the same year, on July 28, 1928, another plane, flying an air route test, a trimotor wooden wing Fokker, on a similar run from Havana to Miami, 'lost' Florida by a 50 per cent compass variation and came down into the sea with loss of plane, mail, and passengers, although the pilots and radio operator survived to tell of the unusual compass deviation.

During the thirties and early forties frequent malfunction of compasses and flight instruments as well as the un-explained disappearances of planes (including two military flights that lost five planes each, from Bermuda to the Euro-pean theater in World War II) were not specifically con-sidered as an area phenomenon until sometime after December 5, 1945, when the now well-known incident of Flight 19 captured public attention. This was the flight of five Marine Air Force bombers on a routine training mission from Fort Lauderdale, in peacetime, months after the end of World War II, which vanished in flight while in 'one way' contact with their base, followed by the dis-appearance of a search and rescue plane dispatched to the area from where the five bombers were still sending messages.

Although at the time of the loss press coverage and general reaction were simply that this was an unusual tragedy that would eventually be explained, this incident, nevertheless, has grown more mysterious with the passage of time, and despite numerous official 'final' explanations nothing definite about the fate of the planes has ever been proved nor has any vestige of the aircraft or pilots been found.

The mass disappearance of the planes of Flight 19, followed by that of the rescue plane and subsequently the disappearance of a number of other military and commer-cial flights in the area, suggested to observers that some-thing very unusual, aside from compass deviations and occasional malfunction of instruments, was present and operating in an area encompassing the waters off the south-

eastern coast of the United States, the northern part of the
Caribbean, the Bahamas, and Bermuda. Gradually pilots,
shipmasters, crews, and the concerned and curious came
to a realization that the majority of the mysterious occurrences of past legend and fact seemed to have taken place
in the same general area, probably caused by the same as
yet unidentified forces. As a result, in the more than thirty-
year period since 1945, the area and its losses have been
subject to more careful scrutiny, and disappearances of
planes, ships, and people have been catalogued and studied
in considerable detail.

We do not know whether the area where the disappearances have occurred and are occurring is truly a triangle, a
rectangle, or trapezoid, although it does seem, according to
its certain key points, to be roughly triangular in shape.
Some of the plane and ship positions catalogued on the map
reproduced in the illustrated section also seem to be outside the 'Triangle' area. Generally, however, such craft
were heading into the Triangle, and the position plotted
marks the last place that any message was received from
them.

The following list, numbered to show the approximate
position of the lost ship or plane on the map mentioned
above will serve to indicate where many of the vessels or
planes were last heard from before they disappeared within the general confines of the Bermuda Triangle. While
many of these missing craft have been the subject of volu-
minous documentation, other, unpublicized disappearances
and new information about previously discussed disappearances have since come to light as a result of increasing
public awareness of what we may call the Bermuda Triangle phenomenon. Consideration of an expanded list of
disappearances offers an opportunity to reevaluate some of
the information we have on hand as to the suddenness and
the attendant circumstances encountered by the vanishing
ships and planes as well as the crews and passengers who
disappeared off their ships, which later were found floating
as derelicts.

NUMBER	DATE	VESSEL	COURSE OR LAST POSITION	NUMBER OF PEOPLE ON BOARD (IF KNOWN)
1	1800	U.S.S. *Pickering*	Guadeloupe to Delaware	90
2	1814, October	U.S.S. *Wasp*	Caribbean	140
3	1824	U.S.S. *Wildcat*	Cuba to Tompkins Island	14
4	1840	*Rosalie* (found abandoned except for a canary)	France to Cuba	—
5	1843, March	U.S.S. *Grampus*	Off St Augustine	48
6	1854	*Bella* (schooner, abandoned)	West Indies	—
7	1855	*James B. Chester* (found abandoned)	Southwest of Azores	—
8	1872, December	*Mary Celeste* (brigantine)	North of Azores	10
9	1880, January	H.M.S. *Atalanta* (training ship)	Bermuda to England	290
10	1881, August	Unidentified schooner found abandoned and later lost again by *Ellen Austin*	West of Azores	—
11	1902, October	*Freya* (bark, found abandoned)	Cuba to Chile	—
12	1908, January 22	*Baltimore* (bark)	East of Hampton Roads, Virginia	9

NUMBER	DATE	VESSEL	COURSE OR LAST POSITION	NUMBER OF PEOPLE ON BOARD (IF KNOWN)
13	1908, January 27	George R. Vreeland (schooner)	East of Hampton Roads, Virginia	7
14	1909, September 18	George Taulane Jr (schooner)	East of Georgia coast	7
15	1909, November	Spray (world-circum-navigating yawl)	Miami to West Indies	1
16	1909, December 16	Martha S. Bement (schooner)	East of Jacksonville, Florida	7
17	1909, December 18	Maggie S. Hart (schooner)	East of Jacksonville, Florida	8
18	1909, December 23	Auburn (schooner)	East of Jacksonville, Florida	9
19	1909, December 25	Anna R. Bishop (schooner)	East of Jacksonville, Florida	7
20	1910, March	U.S.S. Nina (first steamship to vanish)	South of Savannah, Georgia	—
21	1910, March 26	Charles W. Parker (steamship)	East of southern Jersey coast	17
22	1913, December 17	George A. Lawry (schooner)	East of Jacksonville, Florida	6

NUMBER	DATE	VESSEL	COURSE OR LAST POSITION	NUMBER OF PEOPLE ON BOARD (IF KNOWN)
23	1914, January 29	Benjamine F. Poole (schooner)	East of Wilmington, North Carolina	8
24	1914, February 27	Fitz J. Babson (schooner)	East of Jacksonville, Florida	7
25	1915, April	Bertha L. Basker (freighter)	New York to St Martin	—
26	1915, April	Silva (freighter)	New York to Netherlands Antilles	—
27	1915, April 20	Maude B. Krum (schooner)	East of St Andrews, Florida	7
28	1916, November 13	Brown Bros (bark)	East of Savannah, Georgia	12
29	1917, March 6	Timandra (freighter)	East of Norfolk, Virginia	19
30	1918, March	U.S.S. Cyclops (Navy collier)	Barbados to Baltimore, Maryland	308
31	1919, January 4	Bayard Hopkins (schooner)	East of Norfolk, Virginia	6
32	1920, February 10	Amelia Zeman (schooner)	East of Norfolk Virginia	9
33	1920	Hewitt (sulfur transport)	New York to Europe through Triangle	—

NUMBER	DATE	VESSEL	COURSE OR LAST POSITION	NUMBER OF PEOPLE ON BOARD (IF KNOWN)
34	1921, January	Carroll A. Deering (found abandoned except for two cats)	Cape Hatteras	—
35	1921, October 27	Bagdad (schooner)	Off Key West, Florida	8
36	1921	Monte San Michele (steamship)	New York to Europe through Triangle area	—
37	1921	Esperanza de Larrinaga (steamship)	New York to Europe through Triangle area	—
38	1921	Ottawa (tanker)	New York to Europe through Triangle area	—
39	1921	Hewitt (sulfur transport)	New York to Europe through Triangle area	—
40	1921	Steinsund (cargo ship)	New York to Europe through Triangle area	—
41	1921	Florino (cargo ship)	New York to Europe through Triangle area	—
42	1921	Svartskog (cargo ship)	New York to Europe through Triangle area	—
43	1921	Albyan (bark)	New York to Europe through Triangle area	—

NUMBER	DATE	VESSEL	COURSE OR LAST POSITION	NUMBER OF PEOPLE ON BOARD (IF KNOWN)
44	1921	*Yute* (steamship)	New York to Europe through Triangle area	—
45	1922, February 11	*Sedgwick* (schooner)	East of Charleston, South Carolina	6
46	1925	*Raifuku Maru* (freighter)	East of Bahamas	—
47	1925	*Cotopaxi* (cargo ship)	Charleston, South Carolina, to Havana	—
48	1926	*Porta Noca* (passenger ship)	Between Isle of Pines and Grand Cayman	—
49	1926	*Suduffco* (freighter)	South from Port Newark	29
50	1931	*Stavanger* (freighter)	South of Cat Island, Bahamas	43
51	1931, June	*Curtis Robin* (aircraft)	Off Palm Beach, Florida	2
52	1932, April	*John & Mary* (schooner, found abandoned)	50 miles south of Bermuda	—
53	1935, December	*Wright Whirlwind* (aircraft)	Havana to Isle of Pines	3
54	1938, March	*Anglo Australian* (freighter)	Southwest of Azores	39
55	1940, February	*Gloria Colite* (schooner, abandoned)	200 miles south of Mobile, Alabama	—
56	1941, November	*Proteus* (freighter,	St Thomas to Norfolk, Virginia	—

NUMBER	DATE	VESSEL	COURSE OR LAST POSITION	NUMBER OF PEOPLE ON BOARD (IF KNOWN)
57	1941, December	*Nereus* (freighter, sister ship of *Cyclops*)	St Thomas to Norfolk, Virginia	—
58	1941	*Mahukona* (freighter, renamed *Santa Clara*)	600 miles east of Jacksonville, Florida	—
59	1942, November	*Paulus* (passenger ship)	West Indies to Halifax	—
60	1943	*Martin Mariner*	150 miles south of Norfolk, Virginia	19
61	1944	*Rubicon* (freighter, abandoned except for a dog)	Off Florida coast	—
62	1945, January 20	*B-25* (aircraft)	Between Bermuda and Azores	9
63	1945, July 18	PB-4YW (aircraft)	Between Miami and Bahamas	15
64	1945, December 5	5 TBM Avenger torpedo bombers (Flight 19)	225 miles northeast of Fort Lauderdale, Florida	14
65	1945, December 5	*Martin Mariner* (flying boat, rescue mission for Flight 19)	225 miles northeast of Fort Lauderdale, Florida	13
66	1945, December 27	*Voyager II* (schooner)	Coastal waterway	4
67	1945, December 27	*Valmore* (schooner)	Off North Carolina coast	4

NUMBER	DATE	VESSEL	COURSE OR LAST POSITION	NUMBER OF PEOPLE ON BOARD (IF KNOWN)
68	1946, December 2	City Belle (schooner, found abandoned)	300 miles southeast of Miami, Florida	22
69	1947, December 5	C-54 Superfortress (aircraft)	100 miles off Bermuda	—
70	1948, January 30	Star Tiger (Tudor IV) (aircraft)	Northeast of Bermuda	31
71	1948, January 31	Sam Key (Liberty ship)	Northwest of Azores	43
72	1948, March 5	Al Snyder (cabin cruiser and skiff, found abandoned)	Sandy Key and Rabbit Key	3
73	1948, April	Wild Goose (vessel in tow)	Tongue of the Ocean	4
74	1948, December 28	DC-3 (passenger plane)	50 miles from Miami, Florida	35
75	1949, January 17	Star Ariel (Tudor IV, sister ship of Star Tiger) (aircraft)	Between Bermuda and Jamaica	20
76	1949, January 19	Driftwood (fishing boat)	Between Fort Lauderdale, Florida, and Bimini	5
77	1950, March	Globemaster (aircraft)	Northern edge of Triangle	—

NUMBER	DATE	VESSEL	COURSE OR LAST POSITION	NUMBER OF PEOPLE ON BOARD (IF KNOWN)
78	1950, June	*Sandra* (freighter)	Between Jamaica and Maracaibo	15
79	1951, November 4	*Saõ Paulo* (Brazilian cruiser in tow; 20,000 tons)	Southwest of Azores	8
80	1952, February 2	*York Transport* (aircraft)	Northwest of Bermuda	39
81	1952, April	Navy PBY (aircraft)	East of Jamaica	8
82	1954, October 30	U.S. Navy Constellation (aircraft)	North of Bermuda	42
83	1954, December 5	*Southern Districts* (tanker)	Off Carolina coast	23
84	1955, January	*Home Sweet Home* (schooner)	Bermuda to Antigua (through Sargasso Sea)	7
85	1955, September	*Connemara IV* (yacht)	400 miles southwest of Bermuda	—
86	1956, April 5	B-25 converted to cargo (aircraft)	Southeast of Tongue of the Ocean	3
87	1956, July	*Bounty* (schooner)	Between Miami, Florida, and Bimini	4
88	1956, November 9	U.S. Navy P5M (aircraft)	Approximately 300 miles south of Bermuda	10

NUMBER	DATE	VESSEL	COURSE OR LAST POSITION	NUMBER OF PEOPLE ON BOARD (IF KNOWN)
89	1958, January 1	Revonoc (yacht)	Between Key West and Miami, Florida	5
90	1961, April 25	Calista III (ketch)	Bahamas to North Carolina	5
91	1962, January 3	Air Force KB-50 (aircraft)	East of Langley Field, Virginia	8
92	1962	Windfall (schooner)	Off Bermuda	—
93	1962	Evangeline (schooner)	Miami, Florida, to Bahamas	—
94	1963, February 2	Marine Sulphur Queen (freighter)	Straits of Florida	39
95	1963, July 2	Sno'Boy (fishing boat)	Kingston to North East Cay, southeast of Jamaica	40
96	1963, August 28	2 Air Force KC-135 jets	300 miles southwest of Bermuda	11
97	1963, September 22	C-132 Cargomaster (aircraft)	West of Azores	10
98	1964, April	Scuba divers	East of San Salvador drop-off	2
99	1965, June 5	Air Force cargo plane C-119	Homestead Air Force Base to Grand Turk	10
100	1965, October 28	El Gato (houseboat)	Between Great Inagua and Grand Turk	1

NUMBER	DATE	VESSEL	COURSE OR LAST POSITION	NUMBER OF PEOPLE ON BOARD (IF KNOWN)
101	1966, November 1	*Southern Cities* (tug)	Between Freeport, Texas, and Tuxpan, Mexico	6
102	1966, December	*Piper Cherokee* (aircraft)	Between Bimini and Miami, Florida	2
103	1967, January 11	Chase YC-122 (aircraft)	Between Palm Beach, Florida, and Grand Bahama	4
104	1967, January 14	Beechcraft Bonanza (aircraft)	Off Key Largo	4
105	1967, March 23	Beechcraft twin engine (aircraft)	Jamaica to Nassau	2
106	1967, October	Twin Engine (aircraft)	Off Great Inagua	2
107	1967, December 22	*Witchcraft* (cabin cruiser)	1 mile off Miami, Florida, at Buoy No. 7	2
108	1968, April 5	*Elizabeth* (freighter)	Windward Passage	—
109	1968, October 11	*Ithaca Island* (freighter)	Norfolk, Virginia, to England, Western Atlantic	29
110	1969, June 6	Cessna 172 (aircraft)	Vicinity Grand Turk, Bahamas	2
111	1969, July 10	*Teignmouth Electron* (catamaran); (four other yachts found abandoned at same time in same general area)	700 miles west of Azores	—

NUMBER	DATE	VESSEL	COURSE OR LAST POSITION	NUMBER OF PEOPLE ON BOARD (IF KNOWN)
112	1969, August 4	Great Isaac Light (two lighthouse keepers disappeared, their launch still in place)	Great Isaac, Bahamas	2
113	1969, November 4	Southern Cross (yacht)	Off Cape May	—
114	1970, April	Milton Iatridis (freighter)	New Orleans, Lousiana, to West Africa	30
115	1971, September	Phantom II F4 jet (aircraft)	85 miles southeast of Miami, Florida	—
116	1971, October 9	Caribe (freighter)	Colombia to Dominican Republic	28
117	1971, October 31	Lucky Edur (fishing boat, found abandoned)	Off south Jersey coast	10 (estimated)
118	1971, December	Scuba divers	Western shelf of Tongue of the Ocean	2
119	1972, March 19	Scuba diver disappeared from diving boat	Off Fort Lauderdale, Florida	1
120	1973, March 2	Scuba divers	Pigeon Island off coast of St Lucia	3
121	1973, March 21	Anita (freighter)	East of Norfolk, Virginia	32

NUMBER	DATE	VESSEL	COURSE OR LAST POSITION	NUMBER OF PEOPLE ON BOARD (IF KNOWN)
122	1973, March 22	Defiance (yacht, found abandoned and adrift but then lost)	North of Santo Domingo	4
123	1973, May 25	Navion 16 (aircraft)	Between Freeport and West Palm Beach, Florida	2
124	1973, July 17	Haitian refugee ship (in convoy)	Old Bahama Channel	45
125	1973, August 10	Beechcraft Bonanza (aircraft)	Between Fort Lauderdale, Florida, and Great Abaco	4
126	1973, November	PBM Martin Mariner (aircraft)	150 miles south of Norfolk, Virginia	19
127	1973, December 19	Lake amphibian (aircraft)	Nassau–Fort Lauderdale, Florida	2
128	1974, February 26	P-3 Orion (balloon)	1000 miles west of Canary Islands	1
129	1974, April 27	Saba Bank (yacht)	Nassau to Miami, Florida	4
130	1974, July 14	Cherokee Six (aircraft)	West Palm Beach, Florida, to Bahamas	6
131	1974, July 24	Dutch Treat (yacht)	Cat Cay to Miami, Florida	—

NUMBER	DATE	VESSEL	COURSE OR LAST POSITION	NUMBER OF PEOPLE ON BOARD (IF KNOWN)
132	1975, March 27	Lockheed Lodestar (aircraft)	Between Grand Cayman and Fort Lauderdale, Florida	4
133	1975, April 22	Dawn (shrimp boat)	East of Florida Keys, Smith Shoals Light	3
134	1975, April 30	Magnum (outboard, found abandoned, motor running)	20 miles off West End, Bahamas	—
135	1975, June 24	Meridan (sailing vessel)	Between Bermuda and Norfolk, Virginia	5
136	1975, June 27	Ketch	North of Bermuda	5
137	1975, August 4	Twin Beechcraft (aircraft)	West of Great Inagua, Bahamas	3
138	1975, November 9	Oceangoing speedboat	Bimini to Miami, Florida	3
139	1975, December 2	Boundless (oceangoing tug)	Miami, Florida, to San Juan	5
140	1975, December 10	Speed Artist (coaster)	Barbados to Guadeloupe	5
141	1975, December 18	Imbross (tanker)	Off Florida coast en route to Canada	22
142	1975, December	Drosia (freighter)	Off Cape Hatteras	—
143	1976, April	High Flight (motor sailer)	Miami, Florida, to Bimini	—

The number of disappearances catalogued above is still necessarily incomplete, since it does not include certain military and naval planes and other surface craft which are still figuring in investigations of piracy, hijacking, or politico-revolutionary activity. In the last case, one of the above disappearances (No. 124) may belong to this category as a victim of political recapture, while various other cases of refugee ships from Cuba may have either been recaptured or vanished without trace for another reason. Other suspected hijackings of yachts and smaller planes by 'sign on' crews or pirates for the purpose of drug running in Caribbean waters may still be quietly under investigation, with the expectation of locating the missing aircraft or yacht, with modified markings and its new owner, at a port or airfield far from its original destination.

For the above reasons a number of disappearances occur that are not reported. Mel Fisher, head of a Florida treasure diving company, who scientifically scouts the coastal waters with a magnetometer for concentrations of metal before sending his divers down, has located small planes on the bottom, sometimes with the recently drowned pilots still sitting at the controls. Some of these planes, incidentally, had not previously been listed as missing.

While the above list has also indicated the locations where certain scuba divers have disappeared, it is with the full realization that scuba divers have disappeared quite suddenly from a variety of causes, including diver miscalculation, currents in underwater caves, and roving examples of hungry local fauna. The disappearances of divers mentioned in the above list, however, contain certain elements of mystery in that they vanished from clear water not far from their diving boat: David La France (No. 119) while checking his boat's bottom; Ann Gunderson and Archie Forfar (No. 118) off Andros Reef, watched by support divers in their descent of no return; and Dr Morris, his wife, and a guest (No. 120) disappeared while diving from their boat off St Lucia.

With the suspicion that forces, natural or contrived, seem

to be operating within the confines of the Bermuda Triangle, other unexplained disappearances of scuba divers, swimmers, people from beaches, and lighthouse keepers from their posts (No. 112) are beginning to be considered related incidents, as evidenced rather convincingly by the Prime Minister of Grenada in his recent speech to the United Nations General Assembly (page 94). These disappearances of people, without connection of loss of aircraft, ship, or boat, include the numerous instances of large and small drifting craft found without passengers or crew, presenting in turn a further mystery. For, if planes and ships perhaps sailed into an area of destructive vortex or even disintegration, one wonders how ships could survive and only the people disappear.

An answer to the above has been suggested by one psychiatrist and, independently, by interested psychic investigators, that perhaps, as some force or tangible or intangible menace increased in the vicinity of the vessel, the occupants would be impelled, through increasing fear, to throw themselves into the sea. A quotation from Shakespeare, taken from the same scene in *The Tempest* where he refers to the 'vexed Bermoothes,' contains a passage oddly reminiscent of the disappearances of passengers from their ships:

> Not a soul but felt a fever of the mad, and
> play'd some tricks of desperation. All but
> mariners plung'd into the foaming brine and
> quit the vessel ...

an instance where sailors' tales presumably recounted to Shakespeare in the beginnings of modern seafaring parallel the disappearances which are still taking place.

Another curious aspect of ship disappearances in the Triangle is the apparent fact that a negligible amount of them have have sent, or have been able to send, SOS messages. It would be more understandable that explosions while airborne would interfere with a Mayday message from a plane, but oceangoing tankers would presumably have a greater opportunity to send messages, a fact amply proved during sudden torpedo attacks from submarines in wartime. One is led to conclude that it is highly improbable that so many recorded disappearances could have taken place without an SOS message being sent from a ship and, to a lesser extent, a Mayday call from a plane. The often reported incident of the disappearance of a craft after a routine check-in message has largely contributed to the general realization that there exists a perplexing and menacing mystery within this area. One is inclined to conclude that whatever happened to the doomed aircraft or ships happened so suddenly that there was no time to send a call for assistance. The few messages that have been received are so unusual that they have generally been denied or discounted.

Another possibility would be, of course, that sudden interference would make radio communication impossible or inoperative, a feature that has been notably observed on planes and ships that have experienced other elements of magnetic electronic aberration sporadically present in the Bermuda Triangle. Personnel on such craft have noted malfunction of instruments, spinning of compasses, loss of control of craft, power failure, a 'white-out,' or unusual glowing fog, but in spite of these occurrences were able to leave the area and ultimately regain control of their craft.

If these radio cutoffs and compass and instrument malfunctions occurred in only one section of the Triangle, one might conclude that a source of considerable magnetic force was located at a specific area of the sea bottom, as has been noted to exist on land and underwater in certain other parts of the world. But within the uncertain waters of the Triangle the area of anomaly seems to express itself in different areas at different times – a factor that might be a key to the mystery of the Bermuda Triangle.

CHAPTER THREE

MESSAGES FROM THE MISSING
(AND THE ALMOST MISSING)

When we attempt to assess possible reasons for the disappearances and perhaps a unifying series of circumstances
that characterize them, an examination of the last messages
received from some of the ships and planes should provide
us with at least some clues considering the notable lack of
wreckage or survivors.

But it is these very messages that compound the mystery
of the vanishing ships and planes. In many cases there have
been no messages at all; in others, both for air and surface
craft, the last messages received have been oddly deceptive
in that conditions were reported as being satisfactory or
normal – except that the craft never reached their destinations.

'Last messages' from planes and ships that were to vanish
without trace can be divided into routine communications
that gave no hint of impending disaster, and those that expressed surprise, bewilderment, or fear without specifying
the source of the danger that confronted them which the
shipmasters evidently did not completely perceive or recognize. To the former category belongs the DC-3, a chartered
passenger plane approaching Miami for a landing (No. 74
on the map of disappearances), whose pilot announced, 'We
are approaching the field ... We can see the lights of Miami
now. All's well. Will stand by for landing instructions ...'
before he and his plane and passengers disappeared from
the sky.

Several British commercial passenger planes also sent
reassuring communications before they disappeared for-

ever. The Tudor IV *Star Tiger* (No. 70) and its sister ship the *Star Ariel* (No. 75) were two of these. The *Star Tiger*'s official message was: 'Weather and performance excellent. ... Expect to arrive on schedule.' The message from the *Star Ariel* included: '. . . We have reached cruising altitude. Fair weather. Expected time of arrival Kingston as scheduled. I am changing radio frequency to pick up Kingston . . .'

In the case of the *Star Tiger* two rather mysterious radio messages were later picked up. One was received by several ham operators in Morse code spelling out 'tiger' and a spoken message wherein a voice repeated the call letters of the plane – G A H N P. This was received only by a Coast Guard station in Newfoundland. Both these messages were weak and there was, of course, no indication that they were, in effect, coming from the *Star Tiger*, which in any case would have run out of fuel several hours previous to each message. The messages, therefore, only serve to compound the mystery.

Large and small ships have sent routine messages and subsequently disappeared. The *Anglo Australian* (No. 54) radioed 'all well' before it vanished. The famous racing yachtsman Harvey Conover sent a cheerful last message from the *Revonoc* (No. 89), coming through the Florida Keys, to his yacht club stating that he would arrive in forty-five minutes as well as the request: 'Save me a place at the bar.' He did not appear – that day or ever.

While some messages from planes or ships are interrupted or blocked out, other messages are received so long after they could logically have been sent (as in the case of the *Star Tiger*) that they have usually been discounted or thought to be the work of hoaxers. The oceangoing freighter *Anita* (No. 121), although lost and presumably sunk in the northern part of the Bermuda Triangle off Norfolk on March 21, 1973, was nevertheless reported as still sending messages from shipboard a day later. After the U.S. Navy submarine *Scorpion* disappeared on May 21, 1968, on a return trip to Norfolk, Virginia, secret Navy code signals were received on the special VLF (very low frequency) channel. These signals were triangulated by the Navy to reveal the spot on the ocean floor from which they were coming. Nothing was located there. When the *Scorpion* was later located on the ocean floor by the *Mizar*, a Russian Navy research ship, it was at a point four hundred miles southwest of the Azores, hundreds of miles from the location from which the first signals had come. John Keel, an investigator of disappearances (and unusual appearances) throughout the world, makes a trenchant observation in commenting on the Navy's claim that the message on the VLF channel was a hoax:

What kind of hoax? Had some enterprising joker loaded a rare and expensive VLF transmitter into a boat together with a copy of the U.S. Navy's secret code book, sailed out into the middle of the Atlantic, broadcast his phony signals, then somehow eluded the massive search fleet that rushed to the scene?

The last messages from surface craft have been few and enigmatic. The Japanese freighter *Raifuku Maru* (No. 46), subsequent to a radio call for help while between Florida and Cuba, sent another radio message: 'Danger like dagger now. Come quickly. We cannot escape,' unconsciously raising the question that since escape was effectively impossible why summon would-be rescuers to share an inevitable fate? Which, in turn, brings to mind the much-discussed 'Don't come after me' message from Flight 19. Another last message, this time from a small yacht, was not properly a last message at all, but simply an observation from on board his new 'unsinkable' yacht *Witchcraft* (No. 107) from the owner Dan Burack, to his passenger, Father Patrick Horgan. Burack, who had gone out to Buoy No. 7 in Miami Harbor to admire the Christmas Lights in Miami, put in a call to the Coast Guard for help because of a damaged propeller. When the Coast Guard cutter arrived, there was no sign of the *Witchcraft* despite an exhaustive search. But the final message or comment came after the first call for help and was delivered as an aside to Father Horgan while he was still holding the radio key down. Spoken in some excitement, the comment was: 'I've never seen one like that before!' – a cryptic and tantalizingly incomplete observation. The Coast Guard, in answering queries about what had happened to the two men, subsequently compounded the mystery by stating: 'We presume they have vanished, but not lost at sea.'

Of all the messages received, either specifically sent or overheard from planes or ships that have subsequently disappeared within the Bermuda Triangle, the longest series of communications was received from Flight 19, the five Aztec Avenger torpedo bombers lost from Fort Lauderdale Naval Air Station on December 5, 1945, followed by the Martin Mariner (No. 65) sent out after them on a search and rescue mission. One must remember, in the light of many later occurrences, that Flight 19 was the first known incident of what we may call the Bermuda Triangle phenomenon where a plane or planes in flight had been able to report on the unusual conditions noted prior to disappearing. Certain aspects of these communications offer a coincidental forecast describing features of incidents that would occur to other planes and ships in the future. The messages directly received or overheard from Flight 19 not only furnish a preview of fragmentary reports of later disappearances but also describe phenomena later to happen in the Triangle where observers found themselves in similar circumstances and noted the same anomalies.

These later observers, perhaps because they were merely on the fringe of a magnetic vortex or extreme electromagnetic force (if that is what it is), fortunately lived to tell of their experiences. These experiences, when compared with parts of the radio report of Flight 19, suggest what happens to ships and planes when they chance to fly or sail into a combination of what may be recurring conditions at varying points within the Triangle.

Similarities in the reports from Flight 19 and reports

concerning other 'survival' incidents are thought-provoking:

1. MALFUNCTION OF INSTRUMENTS:

When Lieutenant Charles Taylor, flight leader, first contacted the Fort Lauderdale Naval Air Station on his way back from his mission, his first emergency message* was an indication of malfunction of instruments and loss of direction. Pilots of the other planes in Flight 19 made the same reports and comments, adding that their compasses were 'going crazy.' This malfunction of electromagnetic instruments has been so frequently noted in parts of the Triangle that it is carried on naval and air charts as an area of magnetic deviation as well as a frequent dead spot in radio communication. The spinning of compasses has been noted by ship captains from the time of Columbus and by pilots from the time of Lindbergh.

With public awareness of the Bermuda Triangle other military pilots have furnished reports based on their own experiences in what may be precisely the same area where Flight 19 disappeared. One such incident took place two years before that of Flight 19, when a B-24 piloted by

---

* (Note:) For purposes of reference the first exchange messages from Flight 19 are given here:

LT. TAYLOR (Flight Leader): Calling Tower. This is an emergency. We seem to be off course. We cannot see land. Repeat. We cannot see land.

TOWER: What is your position?

LT. TAYLOR: We are not sure of our position. We cannot be sure where we are ... we seem to be lost.

TOWER: Assume bearing due west.

LT. TAYLOR: We don't know which way is west. Everything is wrong ... strange. We can't be sure of any direction – even the ocean doesn't look as it should ...

Lieutenant Robert Ulmer flying at nine thousand feet east over the Bahamas in good weather suddenly went out of control, shaking as if it were being torn apart and losing, in an instant, four thousand feet of altitude. As the plane would not respond to any control and seemed destined to dive into the sea, the crew bailed out. All but two survived. The crewless plane, however, righted itself and flew, without a pilot, across the Gulf to Mexico, where it eventually crashed into a mountain after its epochal 1500-mile truly 'solo' flight.

Dr Robert Digby, of Lansing, Michigan, then a navigator on the flight, expressed an opinion (*The National Enquirer*, May 4, 1976) similar to those of numerous long-observers of the area:

> In those days we didn't realize there was such a thing as a Devil's Triangle ... But I believe there's something down there, some mysterious force in that area. There is just no logical explanation for what happened ...

It is interesting to note that before he left the plane the pilot set the controls northeast, naturally without any strong conviction that the B-24, which was so far out of control, would be so guided. Whatever guided the plane to Mexico represented a course change to almost exactly the opposite direction.

Instrument deviation has often caused planes to become lost in the Bermuda Triangle area, although most of these planes have eventually found their way back on course. Yachts and ships have been temporarily lost. Freighters, relying on their compasses, have hit sandbanks, and passenger ships have been stuck on reefs while sailing in well-charted waters solely because their instruments ceased to function.

Submarine electromagnetic guidance instruments are sometimes affected as well, which is especially logical if there is something under the water exerting an electromagnetic pull. In February 1955 the U.S.S. *Tigrone*, SSR-419, a reinforced submarine icebreaker, was led by instrument deviation to collide with the only underwater peak in its vicinity of maneuver, which it should have missed by four miles if its instruments had been working.

According to the recollection of Ted Hunt, now of North Bergen, New Jersey, who in February 1955 was a member of the crew, the *Tigrone*, a 312-foot-long submarine with a crew of seventy-four men, was on a training exercise of a type referred to as 'operational readiness inspection' in the southern part of the Bermuda Triangle between Puerto Rico and St Thomas. The submarine was equipped with five different types of sophisticated radar and sonar and was operating within prescribed boundaries, which had been used in other maneuvers, comprising twenty square miles of safe area. The exercise involved the submarine attempting to hide from destroyers. At a depth of four hundred feet the *Tigrone* suddenly collided, in an area tested for submarine safety, with a large, steep reef and came to a crashing halt.

In the words of Ted Hunt:

Our bow was crushed in. Most of the men thought we were sinking. Any normal sub would have sunk, but we were on the only sub in the Atlantic Fleet with an ice breaker bow, and that's why we survived. Later we had inspectors check our gyro compass and guidance systems but there was nothing wrong. What was wrong was that, in spite of everything working, something had caused us to deviate 4 miles off course and hit the reef – the one dangerous point in this part of the ocean. The gyro and compass should be back-up systems, but they both malfunctioned. I could never figure out what happened until I heard this talk about the Triangle and how it affected other ships and planes. All I know is that something made our instruments malfunction and we almost lost the sub.

2. DISORIENTATION:

Lieutenant Taylor and the other pilots expressed a sense of

disorientation and strangeness. Further conversation between the pilots included comments on their loss of direction, the possibility that they had somehow overflown
Florida and were over the Gulf, and were heading back east
over the ocean. This loss of orientation in familiar territory
is a frequent phenomenon in the area, whereby pilots find
themselves over islands to which they had no intention of
flying or do not recognize familiar territory because 'it did
not look like it should.'

In some cases a sense of disorientation and vertigo has
affected pilots at the same time as the malfunction of flight
instruments, although unaccompanied by air turbulence.
The experience of Commander Marcus Billson, presently of
Miami, occurred in the same year as the disappearance of
the Avenger bombers of Flight 19 and in the same area. On
March 25, 1945, Commander Billson was flying a PBM
from Banana River, Florida, to Grand Bahama. (One recalls that the first rescue plane sent to look for Flight 19 was
also a PBM and has been suspected by some theorists of
having exploded during the rescue operation. Commander
Billson, however, is of the opinion that PBMs were not
intrinsically dangerous, nor did they have a bad reputation
among pilots.) Commander Billson recalls:

We were on a night flight about half way to Grand Bahama
when things started to happen. The radio compass started to
circle. The magnetic compass was also spinning. Our radio
became useless because of static. All our flight instruments
went out. The night became very dark. There was no sea,
sky, stars, or clouds – only blackness. I experienced very
violent vertigo, the only time it ever happened to me during
5000 flying hours. We didn't know where we were going so
we turned around and limped back to Banana River, navigating by guesswork. As we approached the Base our instruments came back. I always wondered about this but did
not realize the connection until the Bermuda Triangle was
made public.

3. ECCENTRICITY OR LOSS OF RADIO CONTACT:

Although Lieutenant Taylor's first contact with the tower was two-way – in other words, he could send *and* receive – this contact, as the emergency situation worsened, became interrupted insofar as the flight was concerned. The tower, however, could still hear the pilots of Flight 19 communicating with each other, speculating on where they were heading, on how much time they could stay in the air without finding a place to land, and also an observation that they had passed over an island they could not identify. At one point radio contact was made with another passing plane in the same general area, piloted by Lieutenant Robert Cox, who offered assistance but who received the puzzling answer, 'Don't come after me.'

The erratic behavior of base-to-aircraft communication within the Triangle has been a recurrent feature and has been frequently noted by numerous other air and surface craft traveling through the area as well. In the case of Carolyn Coscio (No. 110) the communication eccentricity was that the airport at Grand Turk Island could hear what was being said on the plane although the pilot could not hear the landing instructions from the tower. A like incident which took place in Nassau in 1962 also became a subject for considerable speculation. In this case a plane approaching Nassau requested landing instructions from the Nassau tower but was evidently unable to receive them although the tower could hear the pilot's repeated requests. Although flying conditions were excellent that day in the vicinity of the Nassau field, the pilot apparently could not find his way there or locate his position even though he was close by. Again, communication was exclusively one way and after repeated requests for direction the plane's radio suddenly fell silent and the unidentified plane was heard from no more.

Finally, there is the alleged incident of the truncated messages picked up in the case of the Avengers, the FT-FT-FT call letters of Flight 19 weakly received and lost again before triangulation was established. Also, like the case of the *Star Tiger*'s postdisappearance messages, the above were noted sometime after the planes would have exhausted their fuel supply. In these and other cases there exists the possibility that radio requests for aid, influenced by magnetic forces that we have not yet discovered, 'jumped' a certain space in time. This possibility is reminiscent of the incident of a pilot of a U.S. Navy P-2 (see Chapter 7) whose request for help was first received at a period sometime after he sent it, so that when he finally did land, without aid, he was asked if he wished to help search for a plane which, in view of the information provided, made the pilot realize that he was at the point of volunteering to look for – himself!

4. WHITE OR GLOWING FOGS:

A puzzling element taken from last messages received from Flight 19 shortly before the final break-off of communications included the phrase 'It looks like we are entering white water.' This term is usually applied to rapids or, in the case of the sea, breakers – hardly applicable to the situation where a flight of planes was attempting to find the shoreline. It has been suggested that the expression referred to a 'white-out,' a condition where pilots fly through a mist or light fog, sometimes even in relatively clear weather when the sun is shining, wherein the sky, sea, and horizon all seem to blend together in the same white haze, compounding the pilot's loss of orientation and heightening his impression of unreality as he is, for the moment, lost in inner space. Within these mists or light fogs other planes have undergone very peculiar incidents, some of which have already been described in *The Bermuda Triangle* (Panther, 1975). These range from the case of Pilot Chuck Wakeley (November 1964), who noticed on a clear night flight from Andros to Miami that a fuzzy glow suddenly appearing on the right wing of his plane spread to the fuselage, the left wing, and inside to the instrument panel (where his indicators and electromagnetic equipment were totally malfunctioning) until finally he himself began to glow; to several incidents in the Tongue of the Ocean, a one-and-a-half-mile deep between Andros and the Exuma chain, where boats in tow have been covered by a suddenly appearing single cloud or localized fog into which some of the vessels have permanently disappeared with crews aboard (the *Wild Goose*, a sixty-five-foot shark fishing boat), while in another case (the *Good News*, a 160-foot tug) Captain Don Henry lost his tow into the covering fog and pulled it out again after an epic 'tug-of-war,' noting at the time an unexplainable drain of all electric power on board his tug.

These unusual fogs, or 'electromagnetic clouds,' sometimes appear to bend time itself, as, for example, the incredible time gain experienced in flight by Bruce Gernon, Jr (Chapter 7); the ten-minute loss of time experienced by a National Airlines 727 as well as its disappearance on radar for the same period before landing in Miami (page 144); and a recent flight approach apparently 'stuck' in time experienced by a pilot who flew into a single cloud while closely approaching Bimini and on emerging fifteen minutes later, without encountering head winds or other unusual conditions, found himself to be still in the approximately same position he was before entering the cloud.

The 'white-out,' or white waters described by the message from Flight 19, may have had some relation to these other cloud phenomena with the time effect of Flight 19, evidently of more indefinite duration. While there seems to be a recurrent theme running through many of these disappearances or near disappearances, we have as yet no way of ascertaining whether the forces present in the Bermuda Triangle are natural or otherwise; whatever they are, they nevertheless appear to offer what we may call an alternate course to ships and planes traveling within the area at certain points and times and perhaps under a combination of certain conditions, a course that in many cases has proved to be the course or path to oblivion – at least as far as our 'here-now' time-space continuum is concerned.

The suddenness and completeness of the many disappearances have suggested to some investigators of the Bermuda Triangle that extraterrestrial or interterrestrial entities have been selecting planes and surface craft and their occupants for purposes of study or collection or for other reasons, perhaps inconceivable to us at this time. For this reason it might prove interesting to examine the 'missing' list with a view to seeing whether ships with certain specific cargoes tend to disappear, or whether a certain type of plane vanishes more often than others, or even if the missing persons share certain characteristics or belong to specialized fields. The cargoes of the lost freighters such as the *Sandra* (No. 78), with a cargo of insecticides; the *Marine Sulphur Queen* (No. 94), carrying vegetable oils and caustic soda; the *Anita* (No. 121), carrying coal; the *Ithaca Island* (No. 109) – grain; the *Ottawa* (No. 38) and the *Esperanza de Larrinaga* (No. 37) – bulk petroleum; the *Hewitt* (No. 39) – sulfur; the *Proteus* (No. 56) and the *Nereus* (No. 57) – bauxite; the *City Belle* (No. 68) – lumber; the *Elizabeth* (No. 108) – paper; all these fail to indicate a preferential cargo for such 'skynapping.'

However, in examining the list we note a high potential of military and naval vessels and especially aircraft, almost all during peacetime. These range from prop planes through turbojets to super jets and furnish by coincidence a sort of graded sampling of our military aircraft through the decades, with the exception of our space capsules, which, although noting the occasional presence of UFOs, have not disappeared.

If we give free rein to our imagination, as certain investigators of the Bermuda Triangle have done, and tentatively consider the possibilities of spacenapping, it is still difficult to hazard an opinion as to what type of craft or cargo alien entities would wish to collect. There seems to be no unifying factor with possibly one rather disquieting exception – in considering the question whether in the case of planes that vanish from the sky, surface craft that disappear without a trace at sea, and the case of passengers and crews (but not the cargo) that vanish from the decks of ships, there does seem to be one unifying and perhaps special ingredient in all three types of disappearances. This special ingredient is, apparently, human beings.

A considerable percentage of the ships mentioned in the above list have, in effect, been found, but never the occupants. Even animals have been found on board some of the derelicts – for example, on the *Rosalie* (No. 4) there was a canary; on the *Rubicon* (No. 61) – a dog; and on the *Carroll A. Deering* (No. 34) – two cats. None of these, except insofar as they were hungry, indicating that they had not been fed for an indeterminate period, were able to throw any light on the disappearances of passengers and crews.

Although there have been numerous prominent people among those who have disappeared, such as Air Marshal Sir Arthur Coningham on the *Star Tiger*; Harvey Conover, world-renowned yachtsman on the *Revonoc*; a famous jockey, Al Snyder (No. 72); the first solo circumnavigator of the globe, Joshua Slocum, on the *Spray* (No. 15); another would-be global circumnavigator, Donald Crowhurst, on the *Teignmouth Electron* (No. 111); bankers, businessmen, priests, moviemakers, etc., it would be logical to suppose that their collective disappearances, however potentially disquieting they might be to famous yachtsmen or other celebrities, might be purely coincidental and due to causes other than collection by entities unknown of prominent seafaring earthlings.

There are several elements of extraordinary coincidence in the information now available on the lost craft, some more easily explained than others, which border on the parapsychic.

There are some incidents where several craft have been affected within the Triangle area at the same time; not only the case of Flight 19, when the rescue plane vanished along with the five TBM bombers it was searching for when it penetrated the same area, but also the incident when the search pattern for the *Star Ariel* coincided with the search and rescue operation for the surface craft *Driftwood* (No. 76) with no vestige of either ever being found.

The search pattern for the two lost KC-135s (No. 96) coincided with rescue operations for another ship, the Coast Guard cutter *Chiola*, which suffered radio blackout at approximately the same time as the KC-135s met their doom. While it is, of course, natural in storm conditions for several or many ships to be affected, the normal flying conditions at the time of these occurrences preclude attributing such events to inclement weather, but rather to a sudden and unexpected phenomenon.

An incredible series of coincidences of name and structure are connected with the *Cyclops* incident. The U.S.S. *Cyclops* (No. 30), a navy collier with crew and passengers numbering 308, was carrying magnesium at the time of its disappearance in March 1918. Its loss was first reported in the press as a result of German submarine action, although even at the time people wondered about the fact that no single trace of personnel or wreckage was found in the vicinity of its disappearance. Subsequent investigations of German Admiralty records following the end of World War I revealed that no German submarines were involved. During the navy investigation suspicion alternately focused on the *Cyclops'* allegedly pro-German (and apparently insane) captain and/or a reportedly pro-German United States consul, as well as a possibly mutinous crew, a breakout of prisoners aboard in irons, or even a freak wave causing the ship to turn turtle or break in two – certainly a plethora of reasons for a disappearance. The unusual element of coincidence begins in the case with the loss of a British ship bearing the same name in the North Atlantic during the same year. Then, in 1941, two sister ships of the *Cyclops*, the *Nereus* and the *Proteus*, both with cargoes of bauxite, vanished within seventeen days of each other, in November and December 1941, on the way from the Virgin Islands to Norfolk, Virginia. Again it was thought that German submarines had been responsible for their loss, but subsequent investigation of German records revealed the contrary. But another British ship, also called the *Cyclops*, was reported missing in the North Atlantic during this second investigation. This peculiar coincidence of the disappearance of sister ships of the *Cyclops* and ships with the same name suggests a pervasive interest on the part of an earthly (or unearthly) entity in a certain type of ship or name of ship, although the prime suspect in the case, Germany, was apparently not culpable. The question arises: was there anything about the *Cyclops* that was especially different or of possible future interest? An intriguing fact furnishes one more coincidence: the *Kearsage*, another sister ship of the *Cyclops* (but one that did not disappear prior to World War II), was restructured to become the first United States aircraft carrier, a development of technology that was to change the composition of the world's navies and add a new dimension to naval warfare.

Several coincidental premonitions among passengers or crewmen who 'signed off' certain of the doomed flights and saved their lives are of interest not only because of implied precognition but, perhaps in certain sensitive personalities, of the facility of sensing imminent peril. Such may have been the case with Corporal Allen Kosner, a crew member who was scheduled to go on Flight 19. He requested and obtained permission not to go because, as he later said, 'For some strange reason I decided not to go on the flight that day.' Another member of Flight 19, Lieutenant Charles Taylor, the flight commander, had experienced a decided reticence about taking part in Flight 19 (later correspondence from his mother with the next of kin of another victim indicated that on the day preceding the disappearance he had phoned her and expressed a premonition about the scheduled flight). Prior to takeoff Lieutenant Taylor requested the duty officer to assign another lead pilot and to be excused from the flight (definitely not from lack of training or experience, as he had several thousand flying hours to his credit). This request, unfortunately for Lieutenant Taylor, was not granted and he subsequently disappeared with the others of Flight 19.

Another case of premonition before flight saved a photographer named Oscar Barber from accompanying the Chase YC-122 (No. 103), which disappeared on the way to Bimini on a flight transporting cargo to a film location on Bimini.

There is one more coincidence that may have considerable bearing on the whole mystery of the Bermuda Triangle. This is the perhaps not so coincidental presence of another danger area on the other side of the world – off the southeastern coast of Japan, roughly between the Bonin Islands on the west, the Marcus Islands on the east and the Marianas on the south. For many years this area, locally referred to as the 'Devil' or 'Ghost' Sea, has been the scene of disappearances of large and small craft, fishing boats, cargo ships and warships, as well as planes and at least one submarine. These disappearances have closely resembled those in the Bermuda Triangle. The same compass and instrument malfunctions seem to occur along with extremely sudden and severe electromagnetic phenomena, inexplicable time losses or gains, unusual wave action, consisting not only of tidal waves but 'holes' and 'hills' in and on the surface of the sea, indicating unusual seismic action below, and even a peculiarly special attribute of the Bermuda Triangle, the luminous 'white water.'

In the Devil Sea, as well as in the Bermuda Triangle, there have been survivors of unusual incidents as well as intriguing 'last messages' from some of those who did not survive. One such message, reminding one of the theory of planes disappearing into whirling vortexes or energy whirlpools, was received from a Japanese Kawanishi flying boat on patrol over Iwo Jima prior to the American invasion, during a relatively quiet night when no United States planes were noted in the area. As interviewed by Rufus Drake (*The Deadly Mystery of Japan's Bermuda Triangle*), Shiro Kawamoto, at the time of the incident the commander of a Zero fighter wing in the area, recalls that a last message from the Kawanishi contained the sentences: 'Something is happening in the sky ... The sky is opening up ...' before its final disappearance.

The position of the Devil Sea in relation to the Bermuda Triangle is especially intriguing in that it lies almost exactly on the other side of the world from its sinister counterpart. They both are located approximately between 20° and 35° north latitude, and the 130° east meridian runs approximately through its center. This same meridian, when it crosses the North Pole, becomes 50° west longitude and runs through the eastern section of the Bermuda Triangle. In addition, both areas are bounded or crossed by the earth's agonic lines, magnetic paths proceeding from the North and South Magnetic poles, along which, due to variations in the earth's magnetic field, compass needles point to magnetic north and true north at the same time. It is, moreover, curious to note that in the Triangle area the isogonic line runs directly along a geological fault marking the west side of the mysterious Tongue of the Ocean.

If the anomalies in the Bermuda Triangle and the Devil Sea are caused by magnetic forces, one might almost surmise that a great field runs through the huge electromagnetic dynamo we call the earth, an unexplained counterpart to the North and South Poles, which themselves have changed their positions frequently throughout the millennia. There is even a tradition in Chinese mythology that there are east and west terminals on the planet as well as the North and South Poles – an impossible potentiality in physics, although, in the case of these two diametrically opposed 'danger' areas, a rather interesting thought, possibly remembered in ancient Chinese knowledge or conjecture inherited from civilizations 'before history.'

The final question on coincidence arises: are the disappearances in the Bermuda Triangle and the Devil Sea out of proportion to losses in other parts of the world? The answer, if we consider the circumstances of the disappearances, absence of survivors, SOS messages, wreckage, flotsam, or oil slicks, is an emphatic 'yes,' with calculated odds in the Bermuda Triangle of more than a thousand to one against the same number of unexplained disappearances taking place in another specified area of the same size, equally available to search and rescue operations. This does not necessarily mean, of course, that a trip to or through the Bermuda Triangle is any more, or even nearly as, dangerous as taking a Sunday drive on an expressway. It does indicate, however, that unique forces seem to be present there and that at certain times, when as yet unknown conditions coincide, random or selected ships and planes undergo unexpected changes of course and their occupants experience changes of condition which, up to now, at least, appear to be permanent.

Considering the number of disappearances, the extent of time over which they have been taking place and the increasing public interest in the phenomenon, one wonders why more official recognition has not been accorded to the circumstances of the disappearances, why they are not considered as possibly related, and whether they are perhaps even more numerous than the reports at hand indicate.

Finally, if there are special areas where the instruments of ships and planes become affected or where the craft suffer unexpected pulls or interference, there must certainly be numerous cases of 'near misses' which have not yet been made a matter of public record for what may be understandable reasons of security.

CHAPTER FOUR

A COSMIC COVER-UP?

When *The Bermuda Triangle* began to become a matter of considerable public interest in the period starting with the fall of 1974, an unusual phenomenon was noted by radio and TV stations, the press, and the publishers. A surprisingly large part of the volume of letters received from readers and radio and television audiences was not, as might be expected, simply requests for more information, or comments on shows, articles, or the book itself, but rather a series of corroborative reports from people who themselves had experienced aberrations within the area of the Bermuda Triangle and had been cautioned by their superiors not to discuss these happenings publicly. The tenor of such communications from ex-service personnel has generally been: *When I was in the service this thing happened to me (my ship, my plane). We were told by our commanding officer not to mention it to anyone until it had been investigated. I never heard how the investigation came out. I never discussed it openly before but I am out of the Navy (Air Force, Coast Guard, merchant marine) now and when I heard about it on the program (in the papers, the book) I wanted to tell somebody about it.*

These communications have come from ex-service or retired personnel of the U.S. Navy and Air Force in the United States and, from overseas, from ex-members of the Royal Canadian Air Force, Royal Air Force, and Royal Navy, from members of the merchant marines of many nations, individuals now living in many different parts of the world but who have never forgotten their unusual and unexplained experiences in the Bermuda Triangle.

Other reports have come from airline pilots, ship captains, and members of ships' crews or the passengers themselves. Again and again references are made to reports being made and then 'lost' in the files and to the hard-to-evaluate but still logical possibility that an unusual report made by a service individual might have militated against him on his efficiency report. Others have admitted in conversation that they have witnessed phenomena but have not reported them insofar as they did not affect their particular mission as well as a normal desire not to call attention to themselves with reports that might be considered over-imaginative or visionary.

A feature that recurs with some regularity in reports contributed by ex-service personnel is the reference to the ship's log. As course deviations must be entered in the log, as well as any unusual occurrences, it has happened, according to these unofficial reports, that pages have been excised from the log and not returned on orders or request from headquarters, and the incident is thereafter considered no longer a matter for comment or conjecture.

While it should be conceded that naval and air patrol operations must be carried out in secrecy to be effective, censorship or denial of reports of phenomena in this area after the operation has taken place raises certain questions, one of which might be whether this area is an especially sensitive one operationally or whether reports of disappearances and phenomena are censored or denied because there is no way to explain them.

A pertinent example is an incident witnessed by crew members of the Light Guided Missile Destroyer the U.S. DLG-27, in late October 1969. The following is narrated in his own words by Robert P. Reilly, then a petty officer third class, specialty: radar operational intelligence:

It was in the latter part of October 1969. We were returning from an assignment in Guantanamo. We were sailing north of Cuba. Most of the crew do not know the position of a

vessel, but I was navigating and I knew where we were and
that we were in the Triangle. I do not remember the exact
date but I do remember the time – 23 : 45 hours. I was inside
– there were two lookouts, one on each side of the bridge,
which was about 30 feet from the Combat Information
Center. I first realized that something was happening when
somebody called in that the watch on the starboard side had
seen something and then fainted. Somebody else called, 'Do
you have anything on radar? There's something weird out
there!' We went out to see what it was.... It's hard to
describe. It was like the moon was rising on the horizon
except that it seemed a thousand times bigger – like a sunrise – but no light. It was light itself but didn't emit light.
It kept growing more enormous.

How far away was it?
It was coming up on the horizon about 11 or 15 miles. It
was on the starboard side but sort of in front of us. It kept
on growing for about 15 minutes.

What did the crew think it was?
It looked like a nuclear flash but it stayed there and kept
getting bigger. If it were nuclear we would have got it on
our radar which had a range of over 300 miles.

Did the Captain see it?
He was notified. Then the Junior Officer of the Deck gave
the order to turn the ship about. Maybe he thought it was
a bomb. You know the standard maneuver – 'Turn your
ass to the blast.'

How many people saw it? Did anyone take a picture?
Maybe 70 to 100 saw it. Most were sacked out. I would
have been myself if I hadn't been on watch. At first we
were awestruck that we didn't think to get pictures. Then
some of the guys went for their cameras but it was too late.
Nobody stands on deck holding a camera.

Where was the real moon?
In the sky. It was a clear night. What we saw was not the
moon – that's damn sure.

Do you know whether a report was made?
Sure. It was entered into the log. You have to whenever

you change course. But when we got to Norfolk some officers boarded and took the log away. All I saw in the log was the course change. I guess the Officer of the Deck may have kept another log with reasons for the change.

Was anything more said about it?

Sure. We went on to Norfolk the next day. Everyone was talking about it. The Captain called us together and told us not to say anything about it. So nothing was said about it again. I'm sure there's a report somewhere about what happened.

This last paragraph, with its reference to a well-disciplined crew and a trustful confidence in the filing system, may suggest what happens to some of the incidents and reports. When a report of an unexpected incident is too far out to be included in an operations or intelligence summary, it may be put aside for further study and eventually reassessed as to its priority and put back in the files again. In this way, if each of these unusual reports is considered individually and not linked with a frequent pattern, it may ultimately be classified as a nonhappening or a mass delusion.

Personnel on watch on the deck of a U.S. Coast Guard cutter ('high endurance' class) while en route to Guantanamo, Cuba, on October 10, 1973, clearly observed five UFOs flying in V formation in the vicinity of and over their ship. They were disk shaped, fast moving, and changed color in various shades of red and orange as they approached and departed. This unusual sighting, made slightly north of the Windward Passage, well within the bounds of the Triangle, was not entered into the log because of a standard procedure in force to report incidents only connected with navigation and not to comment on extraneous matters such as UFOs or, one might say, not to report anything really extraordinary so as not to complicate the log.

Of the 150 persons on board, only a few, those on deck at the night watch, saw the objects. In the words of a corpsman on watch (name withheld because of active duty status): 'First we were scared. Then we wondered whether we should report it if the deck officer didn't. But we had the feeling that if we said anything the result for us would be something negative. So we didn't.'

Besides huge indeterminate objects, forms, or clouds rising from the sea, sometimes the sea itself in the Bermuda Triangle has been seen to build itself upward to a great height over a large and contiguous area, much too extensive for waterspouts and certainly of a different shape. It is curious that such reports of unusual phenomena, observed and reported by competent personnel, civilian as well as military, have been received by the proper authorities and apparently filed without further comment or investigation.

A sighting of a rising mound of water, resembling a huge cauliflower, was made by pilots of a Boeing 707 on a San Juan to New York flight on April 11, 1963. It was clearly observed, from about 31,000 feet at 1:30 P.M., by the co-pilot, the captain, and the flight engineer, in that order. The location was noted at 19°54′ north latitude and 66°47′ west longitude in the vicinity of the 5.5-mile-deep Puerto Rico Trench. The observers calculated the rising mass of water to be somewhere between a half to one mile wide and with a height of over three thousand feet. As the captain did not wish to vary his schedule or endanger the plane or passengers, he simply noted the unusual occurrence and continued on his flight plan. The co-pilot, however, later checked with the Coast Guard, a seismic control center, and somewhat oddly, with the FBI, but obtained no corroborative reply as to anything extraordinary having happened in the area at the time given. The pilots, for apparently the same reasons as have impelled generations of military and commercial pilots to mention incidents but at the same time to protect their reputations, have preferred to guard their anonymity.

An indication that something extremely unusual did happen in the area within a relatively short time span was received in a letter from a retired Pan Am pilot, definitely not anonymous, sometime after publication of the above incident. The pilot was Captain Raymond Shattenkirk, who noted a similar incident in flight and experienced, like the pilots of the Boeing 707, a similar reticence on the part of the agencies to which he reported the incident to furnish information or even acknowledge that anything had happened.

Captain Shattenkirk is of the opinion that the sighting previously mentioned should be credited to him. 'Unless the phenomenon occurred on more than one occasion, what was sighted on April 11, 1963 really happened on March 2, 1963.' His letter follows:

... I was the first Officer on Pan Am flight 211 March 2, 1963. It departed New York at 1434 GMT and landed at San Juan at 1822 GMT.

While in flight at exactly 1745 GMT at lat. 20 deg. 45 min. North, Long. 67 deg. 15 min. West, Altitude 25000 feet, heading 175 deg. magnetic, I saw on the surface of the sea approximately 45 deg. off the nose to starboard a gigantic white bubble being formed.

It had the shape and symmetry of the white portion of a cauliflower. From a mental comparison of landmarks and their relative size from altitudes of twenty to thirty thousand feet I would state that Idlewild Airport could easily have fit into the dimension of the bubble.

The crew, Captain John Knepper, myself, Third Officer Ralph Stokes, and the Flight Engineer observed this frightening thing for at least three minutes until it then collapsed into nothing more than a large circle of dark blue water without a trace or sign of smoke, steam or debris. It appeared to come from nothing and it reverted to nothing.

I immediately advised San Juan Center on the frequency we were working and requested them to advise the Coast Guard of our sighting. I was told that an aircraft was being dispatched to the scene.

After landing at San Juan, our flight refueled and departed at 1900 GMT for Miami, Florida.

Indeed, Coast had dispatched an Albatross, for I contacted the pilot while airborne and again described what had been seen. His last contact with me by radio indicated that there was no vestige of our bubble.

This is what happened on March 2, 1963.

Later in the following month of April, 1963 sometime after the 10th of April, I contacted Father Lynch of Fordham, the noted seismologist.

Upon my mention of the sighting and the area involved, what had been a cordial conversation abruptly became a quick brush off, a not so polite goodbye and the phone call ended.

His reaction was strange. Could my mention of the 'Thresher' sub along with the other information have caused his unusual behavior?

From that day on I have been highly suspicious that I blundered onto a terrible secret, certainly not one to be known by the public ...

... I am enclosing my time sheet for the month of March, 1963 along with a notation on the reverse side that indicates my call to Father Lynch at the old Fordham number.

Numerous incidents involving naval surface vessels begin with radar, radio, compass, and other instrumental malfunction. According to a crew member, the U.S.S. *Richard E. Byrd*, category DDG–Guided Missile, lost radio contact during a cruise in the Bermuda Triangle in March 1971, with considerable effects on the Navy crew, despite customary Navy assurances that the Bermuda Triangle is only a legend. In the words of Walt Darling, E5 operations specialist, U.S.N.:

... We were en route from Norfolk, Virginia, to the Bermuda Islands. We were out 4 or 5 days, on a training cruise ... getting ready to go overseas. As we sailed east one by one we lost all means of communication. We lost radar first, then air search, surface search, and land. We had no type of radar contact. Nobody was worried at first. Then the scuttlebutt started that we were entering the Bermuda Triangle. The crew members began to talk about the Triangle and to get worried. Then we lost radio communication although you can usually get it on the wide bands – the lower frequencies at 1000 miles, as there are special stations set up at points around the world so that a ship can take, for example, one from France, another from the African Coast, and intersect them and get a fix on where you are. But we could not get anything. The sky was hazy and overcast so we could not get a celestial fix either. The electronic gyros went out. We had 300 men on board. Many of the crew were afraid we were going around in circles and would never get to our destination. Some said now we would find out personally where all those ships and planes had disappeared to since World War II. The men got very nervous but there was no official statement at the time about what was happening. Then after 9–10 days we suddenly got radio contact with Bermuda and came in. The trip usually takes 4 to 5 days. We never found out what was the matter.

A later incident involved the destroyer U.S.S. *Vogelgesang* in 1972. According to crew members the *Vogelgesang*, on a return cruise from Puerto Rico to the United States in March 1974, underwent an unexpected course modification and stopped at sea overnight and part of one day with all electric mechanical systems non-functional, and no power from the boilers. The crew was never told what was wrong; scuttlebutt implied that nobody knew anyway, an observation familiar to service and ex-service personnel. During the night, although the weather was calm, the *Vogelgesang* suffered, according to the crew, strains and stresses almost as if it were being torn apart. No public report has been made of this incident, nor was any explanation given to the noncommissioned members of the crew.

Such incidents are corroborative of the recurrent pattern of power failures, electronic drains, and stresses that occur within the area and often affect large and small craft, military or civilian, and that are, especially in the case of naval craft, normally not offered for public comment or appraisal.

An intriguing theory that a large passenger ship, the *Queen Elizabeth 2*, was affected by the forces present in the Bermuda Triangle while on a cruise on April 3, 1974 (during which all power was lost and the passengers had to be taken off by another ship), was discussed in *The Bermuda Triangle* (Panther, 1975). The official explanation given was that an oil leak in one boiler had affected all three boilers and cut off all power including electricity. But a statement possibly corroborating the presence of unusual conditions was made in a report that a Coast Guard cutter, the *Dakota*, had lost the *Queen Elizabeth 2* on radar at the time of the power failure, although the ship could be clearly seen from the deck of the cutter. This disappearance from the radarscope of the Coast Guard vessel was later denied by the Coast Guard. An unidentified Coast Guard spokesman quoted in *Time* magazine said: 1) It never happened; 2) Even if it did happen 'the momentary disappearance of a ship on a radar screen is a common occurrence, the result of rain clutter, sea "return," or other natural causes.' One might observe first that all disappearances might be attributed to a general category of natural causes, known or unknown, and, secondly, if it never happened, why was it necessary to explain what the cause *could* have been?

A somewhat similar incident happened to the S.S. *Rotterdam* on a cruise through the Bermuda Triangle on October 10, 1975. Like the *Queen Elizabeth 2*, the explanation given to the passengers was one that could be easily understood: water had got into the oil of one of the engines. According to the cruise passengers, 'Everything went out' – the ship's motors, lights, air conditioning, kitchen facilities, and water suddenly ceased to operate at a point six or seven hours approaching Bermuda from St Thomas. Although the cruise was scheduled to visit Bermuda, it never got there. According to Norman Olsen of New York, a passenger at the time of the incident:

The lights simply went out and the boilers stopped; there was no power for water. It was not a question of bad weather. The weather was clear and the sea was unusually calm. There were no other ships around. We simply stopped and drifted north for most of the day. We never heard the complete story of what was wrong. They don't say much about a thing like that.

There have been no cruise ships among the numerous oceangoing vessels that have disappeared in the Bermuda Triangle. It is interesting to note, however, that there are no reports of large passenger liners that have broken down while crossing on the regular route to Europe. Such accidents as have happened, apart from wartime submarine sinkings, have usually concerned rammings of other ships or icebergs (the *Titanic*, 1912; the *Andrea Doria*, 1956) but not a sudden loss of power on a calm sea. Further instances of electronic interference with passenger ships within the increasingly popular cruise waters of the Bermuda Triangle may throw additional light on the unusual electronic and magnetic variations in the area. It is a comfort to suppose that the very size of the cruise ships may ensure a degree of protection from the 'forces of disappearance,' if they may be so called.

Eccentric behavior of radar screens has apparently been corroborated by visual observations in several almost unbelievable incidents allegedly noted by crews of Coast Guard cutters. Richard Winer (*The Devil's Triangle 2*) cites the case of the *Yamacraw*, a Coast Guard cabling and research ship which underwent a rather unsettling experience on August 8, 1956, within the Sargasso Sea.

The Sargasso Sea, north of the Bahamas, a stagnant area marked by abundant surface presence of seaweed and circled by the Gulf Stream and other currents, has long been infamous as an area of lost and abandoned ships often, according to legend, caught in masses of seaweed. The *Yamacraw* at the time of the incident was hundreds of miles away from the nearest land.

Although the *Yamacraw* was in the open sea, the radar operator suddenly detected a large land mass at a distance of twenty-eight miles directly ahead of the ship and so informed the officer of the watch. The officer checked the sightings and compasses and came to the same conclusion. The captain was informed but he did not alter the ship's course. In a matter of several hours the *Yamacraw* found itself approaching an enormous mass that seemed to be land except for its vast height. This massive substance, while impenetrable to radar or strong searchlights, was nevertheless not land, as it seemed to stand *above* the surface of the water and to continue skyward, stretching from northeast to southwest to an apparently great though undetermined distance. The *Yamacraw*, with commendable exploratory zeal, penetrated the dark mass, which tended to cut off all illumination. The high intensity carbon arc lamps became only a dull glow, which one could see only when one looked directly at it. Soon after entering the mass the cutter's personnel began to cough and the engine to lose steam pressure, causing a command decision to turn about and leave the area. With the following day's sunrise the enormous manifestation vanished with no sign that it had ever existed.

A second radar indication of land or ghost land near the Straits of Florida is attributed to a Lieutenant Wissman, executive officer of the Coast Guard buoy tender *Hollyhock*. The difference between the *Hollyhock* and the *Yamacraw* sightings is that, while the *Yamacraw*'s ghostly land sighting had been approachable, the radar 'land' sighting made by the *Hollyhock* seemed to recede as the vessel approached. It happened in August 1974 as the *Hollyhock* was leaving the Bahama Island group and approaching the Straits of Florida. Although the Florida coastline was approximately fifty miles off, the radar showed a land mass ten miles ahead on the ship's course. It was too large to be another ship. It gave radar indications similar to land except that it moved forward in relation to the *Hollyhock*. Unlike the *Yamacraw* incident the mass, whatever it was, was never actually seen by the crew.

Whether these indications of land or tremendous moving bodies that have no concrete existence represent a malfunction of radar, sea 'return,' or radar being affected by special weather conditions, remains a matter of conjecture. It is also possible that the *Yamacraw* sailed into the thick sulfurous results of an underwater volcanic explosion. Although neither of these occurrences found its way into the news media, it is to be assumed that other, perhaps as yet unreported events of this kind have been or will be subject to scientific investigation and analysis.

Unique cloud formations, standing alone in an otherwise cloudless sky, have been, according to witnesses, observed and photographed by U.S. Navy patrol aircraft, although the results of such photography have not been made available either to the original photographer or the public. Jerry Osborn, now of Dallas, Texas, but on Naval Air Force duty in 1966, was a witness, along with eleven other crew members of a Navy P3-A, of an incident involving two clouds more reminiscent of illogical dreams (or nightmares) than of usual nimbo-cumulus cloud formations. Jerry Osborn, no longer on active duty and therefore free to speak, recollects the incident vividly:

I was stationed at Kindley Field, Bermuda, in January 1966. My rank was AX-3, an anti-submarine war technician. On the 16th or 18th of January we were flying a routine patrol mission between Bermuda and Puerto Rico. It was between 1 and 3 A.M.: the night was clear, the flying conditions were excellent. We were about 400 miles south of Bermuda flying at an altitude of approximately 4000 feet.

Suddenly two very unusual clouds came into view at a flying time of about 5 minutes away at our approximate altitude; one was a long inverted triangle 250 to 300 feet long, pointing down while the other had the shape of a well-defined puff, about 150 feet in diameter, hanging above it. Both were luminous. My first astonished thought or comparison was – someone has made a cloud in the shape of a gigantic vanilla ice cream cone and separated the ice cream from the cone.

I had a very clear view of it because I was acting as duty observer and was located in the upper starboard observer's seat. Even so I would not have believed what I was looking at if all the other crew members had not seen the same thing. The two clouds were just hanging there in the empty sky.

As we came closer I noted that the space between the puff and the cone was about 200 feet and appeared to be empty. As we approached, our pilot started to make a pass at it and to fly across it, but just as we began to make a pass and while our photographers were snapping pictures of the crazy formations, an extremely bright searchlight or beam came out of the space *between* the cone and the puff, scanned the area where we were flying for a couple of seconds and then locked in on our plane. It stayed locked in on us for as long as we were there – about 6 seconds. At this point our pilot broke contact; we wanted to put some space between us and whatever was happening. When we returned to base we made a report and turned in all the pictures that we had taken. We never saw them or heard anything more about the report. We later asked our officer about it. He said he did not know anything about it. He did not seem to want to talk about it but said maybe it had something to do with fallout from one of our space shots. That might explain the cloud but it certainly would not explain the bright light that focused on us and stayed on us from the space between the clouds.

Naval craft, especially the slow-moving radio ships that traverse different parts of the world as well as the Bermuda Triangle, have noted the odd atmosphere and the temporary disappearance of bird and animal life in areas of the Triangle during periods of interrupted radio communication and malfunction of other electronic equipment. Personnel have described the sea during these moments as glassy, devoid of life, without the usually present fish or birds, and have noticed at these times the increasing presence of a light fog.

The experience of the Coast Guard cutter *Diligence* is a pertinent example of communications blackout in the area of the Bermuda Triangle in the last part of 1975. The *Diligence* was engaged in following up a report on a burning freighter, when it lost radio and sonar communication and beached itself on the shallow Bahama Banks.

For an hour it remained without radio communication, with the single exception of contact made with another Coast Guard cutter, off San Francisco, 4,500 miles away.

Whether the Navy and Coast Guard consider the area to be one of danger, aside from the magnetic aberrations that are known to exist, no official spokesman will give an opinion hinting at anything unusual. Navy pilots, however, are apt to be less concerned about the normality of the Triangle area.

One cannot fail to admire solo pilots who patrol the area in small planes and who are increasingly aware of the Triangle's reputation. Several years ago a Navy pilot, an American Indian of tribal background, was lost while in radio communication with his base. He appeared to be in some difficulty but did not send an SOS. He was then heard to be singing in another language. A friend, also an Indian, was called to the intercom to listen to this sound. He recognized it as the 'death song' to be sung just before one's death. The plane and pilot disappeared without trace and without indication of what the pilot had noted to impel him to sing his death song.

Since the loss of patrol planes or individual training flights is normally not reported in the press, it is difficult to ascertain what proportion of disappearances is suffered in the Triangle by the U.S. Navy and Army Air Forces. It is perhaps indicative that in 1974 Naval Reserve training flights were shifted to the Gulf side of Florida instead of the Atlantic side, which lies within the confines of the Bermuda Triangle. As was to be expected no mention of the Bermuda Triangle was made in the directive.

There are several understandable reasons for official sources not to release to the press seemingly unrelated incidents which take place on Navy and Coast Guard vessels within the Triangle area. These probable reasons include the following: 1) Some incidents may take place in the vicinity of non-Nato ships or planes with potential international repercussions; 2) other incidents involving loss of communication contact, alteration from flight plan or course might be interpreted as lapses of professional expertise; 3) still others seem so fantastic that they are evidently simply removed from the ships' logs perhaps for the reason that an account of an unrelated incident would endlessly complicate and eventually obscure the report of the basic mission. The following are indicative examples:

In October 1971 a Coast Guard helicopter ship, on maneuvers near Great Inagua, was engaged in tracking a group of Russian and Chinese trawlers and, at the same time, an unidentified undersea craft as well as a plane suspected of being an unidentified rotorcraft, as it seemed to be going too slowly for a fixed wing aircraft. When the plane approached close astern, a bright landing light flashed on and off and then the craft hit or bounced off the sea and exploded in a blinding, brilliant, orange-white fireball, of indescribably greater intensity than what could normally be expected in a ditching. The Federal Aviation Administration, on being questioned, admitted that an aircraft – a Constellation – had been reported missing but gave no information about the flight plan or the location of the explosion (although the spot had been reported by the observing helicopter) and, in fact, was not sure that the plane or flight under discussion even existed. Subsequently the investigation initiated by the National Transportation Safety Board was eventually dropped and all records classified.

Sometimes reports of unnatural (at least to the observer) happenings in the area are deleted or otherwise suppressed presumably because their publication would open up new and difficult investigations not related to the mission in question. Such a case concerned the well-known DSRV (Deep Submergence Research Vessel) *Alvin*:

Question: *How deep were you when you saw the monster?*
We were down about 5000 feet and then I went down into a crevasse about 300 feet deeper under a slight outcrop. We went deeper because the cable we were following spanned the crevasse. It was right there that I spotted it. The first

thing I noticed was the movement. I thought we were moving along the cable and checked for drift but found that the sub was stationary and that it was the object that was moving. It then occurred to me that perhaps it was a utility pole, especially because of its thick shape. I swung the sub in an arc to get a better view along the cable or pole or whatever it was, when I was astonished to see a thick body with flippers, a long neck, a snakelike head with two eyes looking right at us. It looked like a big lizard with flippers – it had two sets of them. Then it swam upwards with its back turned before we could get the cameras angled. They were set to photograph 15 to 25 feet in front of the submarine and the thing had already swum out of the camera angle but was still around.

What did you do then?
I didn't like the way things were happening, so I came up. I couldn't believe what I was seeing but I didn't want to hang around.

Did you report it?
I talked about it. What can you say when you have nothing to prove it? You get laughed off the deck.

Did you enter it in the log?
I entered it in the wet log, but I don't think it was put in the final log. I heard it was deleted by the Navy.

Was this the only unidentified animal you have seen on your dives?
Well, you do see moving shapes and forms. But they are probably large squids and they tend to stay away from the sub. I've made 300 to 400 dives and that was the only time I ever saw an animal like that.

Dr Manson Valentine, who is especially qualified for identifying and sketching animals by virtue of a doctorate in zoology and the fact that he is an artist, drew a picture of a plesiosaurus and, showing it to Captain McCamis, asked him if the animal he had seen looked like the picture. Captain McCamis immediately replied, 'Yes, that's exactly what I saw.'

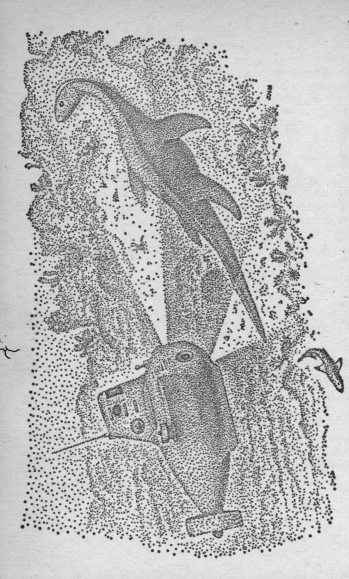

2. Drawing made from description given by Captain McCamis of unidentified animal he reported to have sighted from the mini-submarine *Alvin*, in the Tongue of the Ocean while inspecting cables during October 1969.

It is, of course, understandable that recording officers would hesitate to transcribe accounts of utility poles that metamorphosed into sea monsters, especially if such occurrences were not incidental to the mission in question. However, other fauna of monstrous proportions have occasionally found their way into reports, like the thirty-foot blackfish glimpsed from the PX-15 *Ben Franklin* as it drifted slowly on an underwater exploration tour through the area.

(This same *Alvin* was, on another occasion, attacked by a more explainable example of undersea fauna – a swordfish. This belligerent swordfish rammed its sword with so forceful a thrust between the pressure sphere and the outer padding of buoyant eutectic foam that it could not get its sword free and, as a result, died from decompression as the *Alvin* surfaced.)

The existence of presently unidentified sea monsters in oceanic depths, perhaps living in underwater caverns or crevices such as those in the Bermuda Triangle, is far from incredible and may become even less so in the future as deep sea drilling for oil and submarine patrol activities at increasingly greater depths eventually bring observers into more direct contact with previously unknown forms of undersea life.

As examples of unfamiliar phenomena or fauna are encountered, however, the same problem of making official reports about them will no doubt be repeated. Past procedures in this regard have tended to explain anything unusual in terms that can be easily explained, and, if something is unexplainable – ignore it.

The well-known case of the death of Captain Thomas Mantell, U.S.A.F., occurring as he was in 'hot pursuit' of an unidentified flying object, is a classic example of the 'normal explanation' technique. Captain Mantell, on January 7, 1948, took off from Godman Field, Fort Knox, in a P-51 to establish the identity of an extremely large unidentified flying object in the skies in the vicinity of Fort Knox, clearly observed in conditions of good daylight visibility.

The object was described by the tower as a bright, disk-shaped object, and by Mantell, in flight, as 'metallic and tremendous in size.' Captain Mantell subsequently fell to his death while approaching this object. His plane disintegrated into a variety of small pieces. The wreckage was characterized by being peppered with a profusion of very small holes in the aluminum remnants, none of which were larger than a few square inches. The Air Force explanation of this phenomenon at the time was that Captain Mantell apparently had been chasing the planet Venus (rarely visible in daylight) and then shifted his pursuit to a skyhook balloon (or two skyhook balloons) and then had blacked out because of lack of oxygen and fallen to his death. No explanation was given for the peculiar condition of the surviving bits of plane wreckage.

The same sort of normal, easy-to-understand (although hard to accept) explanation was offered by the Air Force to clarify an incident which took place within the Triangle area on March 9, 1957. A Douglas DC-6A – a Pan American passenger flight under the command of Captain Mathew Van Winkle – was approaching Miami from the north for landing. Captain Van Winkle noticed a bright light traveling at a great rate of speed (he thought it was a jet) about to intercept his course. As it came closer it appeared to be circular, very bright, and characterized by a greenish glow, and Captain Van Winkle suddenly realized that if he continued on course he would meet it head on. In taking evasive action he lifted his plane and then depressed it, causing considerable pandemonium among the passengers, some of whom were slightly injured.

An investigation of the incident involving the Air Force and the Civil Aeronautics Board considered several possibilities, such as jets (none in the area), missile trails (no launchings at that time), and finally that Captain Van Winkle had imagined the whole affair, although it was ascertained that other planes had seen the same glowing object. The final findings were simply that the captain had seen a shooting star!

Often a standard operating procedure, in this case a curtain of silence if not official censorship, falls over an incident or is discreetly drawn over the result of an operation for the calm and well-being of the public. This does not refer, of course, to understandable censorship in times of war. In an effort to keep the first atom bomb explosion at Alamogordo a secret a press release was prepared stating that the blast, which could be seen within a radius of 150 miles, was simply the result of 'an explosion at a local installation.' This explanation, although undeniably true, might also be termed one of history's great understatements. From time to time when unexplainable incidents occur, an effective peacetime censorship slides into place like a well-oiled bolt.

Nevertheless, news of unusual incidents is often disseminated within certain service levels, presumably on a 'need to know' basis, with appropriate threatening warnings applicable to personnel who discuss such matters outside of stated military confines. One such report was circulated in 1960 by the Air Force itself through special units, radar and other, concerning a test flight of an F-101 which reportedly took place in May 1960 at Edwards Air Force Base in California. According to the report, the F-101, piloted by an Air Force major, was being tracked on radar while returning to base after a mission. Suddenly a large disk appeared on the radar screen over the plane's radar image, which was then seen to ascend and blend with the large disk, as if it were being taken aboard, and the large object vanished. An immediate though unsuccessful search was made for the plane, interrupted the following morning when the missing plane reappeared still piloted by the major, who was, understandably, somewhat bemused and vague. He reported being lifted up, together with his plane, *into* a huge UFO where he was allegedly 'interviewed' by humanoids who expressed considerable interest in his test plane. According to his report he and the plane were released some ten hours later and he then flew in to land at his base. Before his 'capture' he had about twenty minutes of fuel left and had approximately the same amount when he resumed his interrupted flight, using the normal amount for his return landing, without counting the missing ten hours. After his preliminary report the major was sent to the psychiatric ward at the base hospital and from there transferred to another point, with no forwarding address made public. All personnel involved in this incident, or even cognizant of it, including those who had read the report, were warned by their COs or appropriate security officers of the considerable penalties, fines, and/or imprisonment for security violations in this matter.

At present such reports are no longer distributed, and strict control of unusual reports and resultant cutoff of dissemination at the source is typical of incidents that have happened and are still happening in the Bermuda Triangle. These include Air Force sightings of UFOs in the sky, under the surface of the sea, and entering and leaving the water, and the active participation of an underwater UFO in a United States Navy maneuver off the east coast of Puerto Rico in 1963, during which it was checked at underwater speeds of up to two hundred knots and tracked to a depth of twenty-seven thousand feet (cf. *The Bermuda Triangle*).

Unusual and perhaps indicative evidence of not only the presence but possibly a hint of the purpose of the many UFOs observed in the area has been the sighting of UFOs by astronauts in the majority of Gemini and Apollo space shots from Cape Kennedy, as well as the tracking of UFOs by ground control. Astronaut James McDivitt photographed a UFO from Gemini 4, and Frank Borman and James Lovell on Gemini 7 observed in detail two mushroom-like UFOs with active propulsion systems and also successfully took pictures of them, as did James Lovell and Edwin Aldrin on Gemini 12. Astronauts Borman and Lovell on Apollo 8 and Stafford and Young on Apollo 10 also took pictures of UFOs while in orbit as well as on their return trip. Apollo 11 was followed almost to the moon (Astronaut Edwin Aldrin was successful in photographing two of them), and Apollo 12 was also accompanied by a UFO during its moon orbiting.

These accompanying UFOs may not always fit the category of simple observers. Maurice Chatelain, a French scientist formerly for many years with NASA, has mentioned (in *Nos ancêtres venus du cosmos* – 1975) the theory that a mysterious explosion in the Apollo 13 service module oxygen tank may have been caused by a UFO intent, for reasons unknown, on inhibiting the accomplishment of the mission.

While it is possible that these reported UFOs are space junk or asteroids, what is apparently certain is the withholding of much of this information from the general public. One need not label this fact of life as a 'Watergate,' cosmic or otherwise, when it is obviously an unwillingness on the part of government agencies to admit that unusual forces are at work within the area, as well as the natural reluctance of individuals to endanger their promotions or their credibility by sticking to their original reports of inexplicable incidents. Nor can one expect commercial airlines, passenger or cargo, to support or supply evidence that something other than normal sudden changes of weather may exist in the Triangle. Nor should we be surprised that official channels neglect to consider the complete absence of wreckage, lifesaving equipment, or oil slicks from the many disappearances as due to anything other than currents or the understandable fact that 'it's a big ocean.'

However, certain elements of security or cover-up connected with the most famous disappearance in the Triangle, that of Flight 19, have suggested to some researchers as well as to various family members of some of the victims, that a continuing censorship has been applied to this incident for a curious and surprising reason.

Although several fact sheets about the missing Avengers postulate explanations such as loss of bearings by the lead plane, which, followed by the others, flew east over the ocean, where it eventually ran out of gas and ditched, leaving no wreckage, survivors, rafts, or oil slicks. The

vanishing Martin Mariner is conveniently explained by the
fact that a flare in the night sky was observed by the crew
of the S.S. *Gaines Mills*, a passing freighter.

The investigation of Flight 19 was classified for some
years and, as late as 1946, nineteen years after the disappearance, the Department of the Navy again issued a
bulletin for answering public queries about the famous
flight. Even in this bulletin it is stated that the evidence
concerning the loss '... is insufficient to determine exactly
what did happen. The flight was never heard from again
and no trace of the planes found ...'

It is nevertheless interesting to note that several incidents
at the time of the loss suggest that there may have been
some survivors from the planes and that they were near
shore or actually on shore or even rescued without such
rescue being publicly reported.

According to Sal Macedonia, now of Madison, New
Jersey, and formerly a radio operator on the U.S.A.T.
Ernest J. Hines, who, by an extraordinary coincidence, took
a photograph, while he was on deck and his ship was
leaving port, of the passing Avengers on what was to be
their last flight. He later heard over the ship's radio that a
search for the five planes was going on and realized that
those were the five planes that he had photographed. About
9 P.M. on December 5 he received a weak call signal in the
vicinity of the search, just several miles off the Florida
coast, not identifiable as an SOS. He is of the opinion that
the call came from a small surface craft, although it could
have come from a downed plane. He reported the matter
but no action was taken 'as the junior officer did not want
to wake up the skipper,' and it was assumed that the search
planes had also picked up the signal. Other reports of
possible land survival came from various sources concerning green and sometimes red flares reported by pilots
in flight (Pan American and Eastern Airlines and a bus
driver) on the night of the disappearance. These flares were
seen at various locations, including the Everglades, the
area around Fort Myers, and central Florida, all indicative

of persons signaling an emergency. Moreover, since the intensive search was called off on December 10 after only four days, it might possibly be assumed that something was found in the meantime to justify its suspension.

The surviving widow of Captain Powers, as recently quoted in *Saga* magazine ('The Greatest Mystery of the Bermuda Triangle,' by Kenneth Woodward), indicated her impression that some of the victims of Flight 19 neither died nor disappeared from the earth and that some of them might be still alive. She bases her opinion partly on her own intuition and partly on the brief extent of the search despite the close-by sightings as well as the report that an offer by the local Seminole Indians to participate in the search was refused, and in view of other reports that survivors had been found on shore in Florida by another government agency and had been sent to a West Coast military hospital. For years Joan Powers has tried to track down these rumors but has generally come up against a wall of official silence. Her explanation of possible survivors and the unavailability of further information is thought-provoking.

'My own theory,' Joan Powers has stated, 'is that the men saw something up there over the Triangle – something strange which jammed their instruments, something which so frightened Lieutenant Taylor that he did not want Lieutenant Cox [to whom Lieutenant Taylor radioed "Don't come after me!"] to jeopardize his own life; something which, possibly for national security reasons, the Navy still does not want the public to know about ...'

When spokesmen for the official organizations that have regional accountability for safety or information touching on the area have been asked their opinion about the possible presence of unusual forces in the Bermuda Triangle, their reactions have predictably ranged from cautious denial to derision.

The Coast Guard offers a prepared fact sheet about the Triangle in which the first paragraph proclaims it an 'imaginary area,' while another paragraph gives its coordinates in case it may not be imaginary. The Federal Aviation Administration, while qualifying the alleged mystery as 'nonsense,' admits that there are special problems associated with flying in the area and suggests that the sudden disappearances of planes are caused by 'neutercanes' – small hurricanes *within* 'harmless rainstorms,' adding perhaps another element to the mystery. Neither the United States Navy nor the Air Force officially recognizes the area as a danger zone, an opinion with which many operational flyers do not completely concur. National Oceanic and Atmospheric Administration officials are not as sure of the nonexistence of the Triangle as the other organizations. A NOAA spokesman, as quoted in *Newsweek*, December 16, 1974, has observed: 'Despite efforts by the United States Air Force, Navy, and Coast Guard, no reasonable explanation to date has been made for the vanishments.'

Individual oceanographers, meteorologists, airline executives, and scientists are more direct. Gene Dubois, of Eastern Airlines, defending the position that airlines will not recognize the area, puts it down to 'sensationalism and nonsense.' Isaac Asimov, scientist and science fiction writer, does not 'think that anything is essentially unexplainable. There are only things that are unexplained. They may never be explained because we may never have the data to explain them with ...' Claes Rooth, oceanographer at the University of Miami, states that he does not know 'of a single documented case where I have to strain my imagination to see a possible natural explanation.'

There has, nevertheless, been some apparent straining of imagination among skeptical observers of happenings in the Bermuda Triangle to justify a number of otherwise unexplainable disappearances.

As one way of giving a natural explanation to the disappearances of ships in the area, encounters and collisions with such acceptable monsters as whales have been suggested. It is a matter of record that small- and medium-sized vessels have occasionally been sunk at sea by whales. The *Essex*, a large whaling ship, was sunk near the equator on November 20, 1820, by a ninety-foot sperm whale, justifiably incensed by the whaler's pursuit and harpoons. More recently an oceangoing vessel on the Rio–Copenhagen run and several yachts, one piloted by Douglas Robertson and another by Maurice Bailey (see Bibliography), were sunk as a result of collisions with whales, whether by accident, unprovoked attack, or perhaps playful bumps from the whale, supposing the hull to be another giant cetacean.

In addition to supposed collisions and sinkings at sea by careless or hostile but still *identifiable* sea monsters, it has been suggested that vessels have sometimes been run down by other ships without the larger ship noticing the incident, a sort of hit-and-run accident at sea. This last possibility was suggested by fellow yachtsmen to explain the disappearance, except for a dinghy in tow, of the *Revonoc*, piloted by the veteran racing yachtsman Harvey Conover, on her way to Miami through the Keys on January 1, 1958. It was supposed that the *Revonoc* had been run over by an oceangoing freighter at night and sent to the bottom in a spiral that would leave no wreckage and that the crew of the freighter would not notice a collision with a small craft. However applicable this theory might be to sailing vessels, it would still not explain the disappearance of freighters which, if run over by other freighters, would undoubtedly be noticed.

While on the subject of 'debunking' the Triangle, mention should be made of a book written by a librarian in Arizona named Lawrence Kusche (*The Bermuda Triangle Mystery – Solved*), which expressed the point of view that the mystery has been solved because there was never any mystery in the first place. It should nevertheless be noted that the author's approach to the subject is not influenced by any personal familiarity with the area of the Bermuda Triangle, the Atlantic Ocean, or any other large body of water. His research techniques are characterized by a somewhat touching reliance on long-distance telephone calls as a means of investigation, as mentioned by him on page XV of the introduction to his book.

As quoted in *The Riddle of the Bermuda Triangle*, by

Martin Ebon, Kusche has observed: 'There was nothing to be gained by my going to the area to do the research.' – a refreshing comment on investigative techniques which would immeasurably simplify the work of detectives, police, research investigators, and explorers throughout the world.

A number of magazine articles have also appeared, pro and con the Bermuda Triangle concept, some of the more critical appearing, understandably, in magazines distributed by the commercial airlines whose routes lead planes through or near the somewhat elastic Bermuda Triangle area.

However, there is no general consensus among oceanographers, scientists, government officials, or anyone else about the happenings in the Bermuda Triangle. At least one government, of the new state of Grenada, located in what was formerly the British West Indies, has recently taken a definite stand on the Bermuda Triangle through its Prime Minister, in an address delivered before the General Assembly of the United Nations.

During this speech, made at the Thirtieth Session of the General Assembly of the United Nations, on October 7, 1975, Dr Eric Gairy, the Prime Minister of Grenada, suggested that:

'The time has come when the United Nations Organization must seriously give thought to, and initiate the establishment of an appropriate department or an agency devoted to psychic research ... man's ignorance of certain aspects of his immediate environs and, most certainly, of his esoteric or inner self, and the various inexplicable phenomena which continue to baffle even the most advanced branches of science. The "Bermuda Triangle" is but one example ... The knowledge that may become available to man through psychic research could very well make him the complete master of self and circumstances, and not the subject, in some cases the slave thereof.'

This unexpected mention of the Bermuda Triangle in the General Assembly of the United Nations received considerable press coverage throughout the world, some foreign press reports stressing that the Prime Minister had asked the United Nations to solve the mystery of the Bermuda Triangle and 'to prevent that men might become, in the future, slaves of circumstances beyond their control,' possibly an allusion to extraterrestrial forces or entities within the Triangle.

Because of the worldwide awareness of the Bermuda Triangle it is interesting and perhaps coincidental that the United States Navy is presently carrying out (1976–77) a joint investigation (project name: Polymode) with fleet units of the U.S.S.R. to study the magnetic stresses and aberrations, irregular ocean currents and waves, underwater sound channels, and suddenly appearing magnetic storms in a section of the Western Atlantic Ocean corresponding to the area of the Bermuda Triangle.

This interest on the part of the United States Government in the Triangle area is reminiscent of the investigations during Project Magnet, a joint Canadian–United Kingdom–United States project terminated in 1956, during which the magnetic aberrations of the Bermuda Triangle were investigated. (It is interesting to note that a Navy Martin Marlin, while engaged in work on this project, vanished in 1956 with all hands while flying in the area, with the usual results of no wreckage, no Mayday, and no explanation of what had happened.)

One may conclude that the participation of the United States in Project Polymode, coincident with the Soyuz-Apollo co-operation, serves not only to point up the interest of the U.S. Navy and oceanographers in 'inner space,' but also an intensified though unexpressed interest in the phenomena of the Bermuda Triangle, which no one in the Government will credit or even mention officially but which Government agencies are evidently willing to investigate. Perhaps this investigation will throw some light on or even explain what happened to some of the ships and planes in this area which have sailed and flown into limbo during the last thirty years.

Although Project Polymode has been announced in the American press in headlines like: US AND SOVIETS TEAM UP TO EXPLORE THE BERMUDA TRIANGLE, one could hardly expect the United States Navy to admit that the Triangle was under investigation although, by an apparent coincidence, the area concerned is roughly contained between the same co-ordinates of latitude and longitude in the Western Atlantic.

While the investigations of the joint U.S.–U.S.S.R. project may or may not discover the reason for the magnetic anomalies, they may face potential encounter with forces within, above, or on the surface of the earth, natural or otherwise, that have not yet been identified.

There also exists the probability that these forces may have been active in this area for hundreds – perhaps thousands – of years and that there may be a connection between the mystery of ship and plane disappearances and another mystery that has obsessed mankind for millennia – the legendary disappearance of a continent.

CHAPTER FIVE

LOST ATLANTIS – FOUND IN THE BERMUDA TRIANGLE?

A drowned empire that has persisted in the legends of the human race as Atlantis may today lie under the waters of the Bermuda Triangle, perhaps a victim, in the distant past, of the same violent forces for which the area is still known. In the same way that the phenomenon of the Bermuda Triangle is generally discounted by physicists and meteorologists and military and civilian authorities, so do oceanographers and archaeologists persist in denying new discoveries in the Triangle area which are indicative of the existence of a sunken civilization. But undersea research, some of which has been given impulse by public interest in the Bermuda Triangle, may have uncovered what may be the first concrete proofs of the Atlantis legend.

We are more or less familiar with the concept of a great lost civilization formerly existing on a continent or great islands now sunk in the Atlantic Ocean. This legend has been preserved for thousands of years for the more imaginative among us, by Plato and other recorders of antiquity, although almost since the time that Plato first reported it, it has been derided by critics and skeptics.

This controversy, which has already lasted for at least 2,500 years and has been the subject of over twenty-five thousand books and countless articles in almost all the world's languages, is still going on today as scientists on various parts of the earth's surface attempt to prove that they have found the civilization before civilization and still other scientists attempt to disprove their findings.

Expeditions probe under the oceans and inland seas,

under deserts that once were seas, on islands that may have been mountain peaks of now drowned land, on mountaintops where the survivors of the cataclysms may have been washed by the tides that swept the earth, and under frozen surfaces of the extreme north and south which once were temperate and livable zones before the poles wandered to their present positions.

Atlantologists, that is, prehistorians and archaeologists or explorers interested in the Atlantis legend, have 'located' the lost empire at a variety of different places on the globe. A sampling of 275 investigators of the subject has produced many different opinions: 46 of the 275 experts are convinced that Atlantis never existed; 131 place it in a choice of 40 early locations, other than in the Atlantic Ocean (and one member of this group places it on Venus!), while 98 think (but so far have not definitely proved) that Atlantis was where Plato said it was – on the bottom of the Atlantic Ocean.

Plato, who described Atlantis in great detail in his *Timaeus* and *Critias* dialogues, was accused at the time of inventing a good story and making it more interesting by claiming it to be factual, attributing the report to Solon, the Athenian lawgiver, who interviewed priests about it on a visit to Egypt. These priests still possessed, according to Plato, written records of Atlantis on the columns and walls of their temple at Saïs, Egypt. Solon's account had been given to Plato's great-grandfather.

Plato identified Atlantis and its age in words that, although written down in ancient Greece 2,400 years ago, still strike a chord of fascination and mystery when we read them today. He tells that '... In the land of Atlantis there was a great and wonderful empire, which had ruled over the whole island and several others [in the Atlantic Ocean] as well as over part of the continent ... They subjected the Columns of Heracles' [i.e., Gibraltar] 'as far as Egypt and of Europe as far as Tyrrhenia' [i.e., Italy] ... 'They had such an amount of wealth as never before possessed by kings and potentates and is not likely ever to be again ... All the outside of the temple they covered with silver and the pinnacles with gold ... The roof was of ivory, adorned everywhere with gold and silver and orichalcum' [perhaps a bronze alloy] ... 'The docks were full of triremes and naval stores ... the entire area was densely crowded with habitations and the canal and largest of the harbors was full of vessels and merchants coming from all parts ... Moreover, there were a great number of elephants on the island, and there was provision for animals of every kind ...'

This pleasant land in Plato's words came to a sudden end: '... Afterwards there occurred violent earthquakes and floods, and in a single day and night of rain ... the island of Atlantis disappeared and was sunk beneath the sea ...'

Plato's detailed account of Atlantis, reputedly later verified by him and some of his disciples who visited Saïs, has since been supported by ancient traditions, shared legends and customs, a worldwide common tradition of a great flood from which only a selected few escaped, linguistic similarities that would be unexplainable except through common contact and pre-Columbian written references on both sides of the Atlantic, all suggesting a continent or large islands in the Atlantic from which civilization was carried to Europe, the Mediterranean, the Middle East, and the Americas. Traditions of a lost continent and contacts with an older civilization remained so strong in Europe *and* the Americas that when the Spaniards began their transoceanic explorations they fully expected to find remnants of Atlantis on the way to a new continent while the Aztecs and other American nations also expected white men or white gods eventually to return from the lost land of their origin, which many Amerindian nations still called 'Aztlán.'

The similarity of names used by ancient races for either a sunken island in the Atlantic Ocean, a Paradise, or a land from whence civilizations spread to an earlier world is a factor contributing considerably toward the theory, although not necessarily a proof, that such a land once existed. The

ANCIENT CULTURE GROUP	NAME OF LOST ISLAND, CIVILIZATION BEFORE THE FLOOD, OR PARADISE	TRADITIONAL LOCATION OR REFERENCE
Greek and Roman	Atlantis	Island civilization in Atlantic Ocean.
	Atlas	Mountain range on Western Atlantic coast, continuing into and under the ocean.
Phoenician and Carthaginian	Antilia Antilha	Island in Western Atlantic Ocean on secret Phoenician trade routes.
Egyptian	Amenti Aalu	Paradise in the middle of the Western Atlantic Ocean.
Babylonian and Sumerian	Arallu	Island paradise in the Western Atlantic Ocean.
Welsh Celtic	Avalon	Island Paradise in Western Ocean.
Nordic	Valhalla	Paradise in the West.
Spanish Celtic	Antilla Atlantida	Island civilization in the Atlantic near Spain.
Berber and Ancient North African	Atarantes Atlantioi	Warlike invaders from northwest Africa.
	Attala	A northwestern sea island, site of a former empire.
Arabic	Ad	The land before the Flood, west of the Mediterranean.
Guanche (Canary Islands)	Atalaya	Sunken Atlantic empire of which the Canary Islands were part but survived.
Basque	Atalaintika	Sunken island in Atlantic from which the Basques came.
Aztec	Aztlán Az	Island with a great mountain in the Eastern Sea (Atlantic Ocean), original home of Aztecs.
Maya	Aztlán Atlán	Former land in Eastern Sea from which the Maya came.
Toltec	Tlapallan	Island in Eastern Sea, home of civilizing gods.
Tribes of North America, Central America, and northern coast of South America	Atlán	Island in Eastern Sea from which tribal ancestors came.

table opposite is indicative of the power of a name and its retention in the history, legends, and consciousness of ancient peoples living in a great circle around the Atlantic Ocean over a period of thousands of years. Although we do not know what the Atlanteans called their land, the incidents of the sounds represented by the letters A, T, L, and N are noteworthy.

An additional reminder of the vanished empire of the sea is furnished by the sound *atl* – 'water' – both in the ancient Aztec language and the Berber tongue of North Africa. There may even be an indication of the name of 'the land before the Flood' in the Bible in the case of the name *Ad-am*, designating the first man or perhaps the first civilized race.

Persistent although uncertain memories of this sunken land lasted through the ages and, in effect, were largely instrumental in inspiring oceanic exploration, especially as certain maps of the Middle Ages, copied from ancient Greek sources, still showed Atlantis or Antilla out in the Western Ocean.

A section of Plato's account, moreover, is especially pertinent to islands in the Bermuda Triangle, the Bahamas, Bermuda, and the Antilles, and was not without influence in the discovery of the New World by Columbus. In describing the location of Atlantis, Plato said:

... in those days [9,000 years before Plato's time or 11,500 years before ours] the Atlantic was navigable, for there was an island situated in front of the Straits which you call the Columns of Heracles; the island was larger than Libya [North Africa] and Asia [the Middle East] put together, and was the way to other islands, and from the islands you might pass through the whole of the opposite continent which surrounded the true ocean, for this sea which is within the Straits of Heracles [the Mediterranean] is only a harbor, having a narrow entrance, but that other is a real sea, and the surrounding land may be most truly called a continent ...

This reference to a continent on the other side of the Atlantic from Europe, recorded two thousand years before Columbus, is representative of a general belief held in ancient and medieval times, a factor that was a source of encouragement to Columbus, a dedicated student of Plato, who was also told by a scholar correspondent before his voyage that he could probably provision his flotilla at one of the surviving remnants of Atlantis. What makes this mention in Plato's account especially relevant in his reference to 'other islands,' indicating a series of large land areas in front of the American continents, which, in order to conform more exactly to Plato's account, should be more extensive and more numerous than those in existence today.

In this connection it must be remembered that Plato referred to a fairly exact period in the past and, whatever the exactness of his information about Atlantis, it is certainly surprising that he should describe islands off the coast of a continent apparently then unknown.

Also, at the time that Plato was talking about, the Atlantic Ocean contained considerably greater land areas, comprising much larger islands among the existing ones, other islands now covered by water, and coastal lands extending far out into the Atlantic. The ocean was then approximately a thousand feet shallower than it is at present, this being before the waters released by the melting of the third glaciation caused the oceans to rise to their present level. Great sections of what is now sea bottom existed as extended coastlines, great islands, and connecting land bridges between the islands. Proofs of this rising of the waters are notably present in the area of the Bermuda Triangle, where the extensive underwater banks of the Bahamas and Florida with their vast underwater caves – the Blue Holes – give ample evidence of having existed for millenniums *above* sea level. A rather convincing indication of the rising of the waters is the presence within the Blue Holes of stalagmites and stalactites (spires and rock 'icicles' formed by drippings from cave ceilings only when caves are above water), coral formations at a relatively great depth (coral normally forms near the surface), the discovery of deep beaches in the ocean (beaches form from waves breaking on the shore), and the results of oceanic probes in the Caribbean (Duke University, 1969) when samples of igneous granite were brought to the surface, indicating continental subsidence.

Underwater probes in the vicinity of the Azores Islands, far out in the Atlantic, have also given results indicating a considerable rising of the waters or sinking of former land areas, especially the retrieval of vitreous tachylyte from the sea bottom, first in 1898, during the repair of the transatlantic cable, and again in 1969 by a Russian oceanographic expedition. The significance of the tachylyte, a basaltic lava, resides in the fact that, in order to be vitreous instead of crystalline, it would have to cool above the surface of the water. In each case it was dated as having been extruded about fifteen thousand years ago. In addition, deep core samples taken from the ocean bottom near the Azores strongly suggest that the material contained in the cores was compacted above sea level.

Calculating a general thousand-foot change in present sea levels and, with allowances for even greater variations caused by volcanic eruptions during the sudden rising of the waters, we can reconstruct, in our imagination, the shape of the Western Atlantic lands about twelve thousand years ago. The Bahama Banks would be above water, a great land area with huge ocean bays such as the present Tongue of the Ocean and the Exuma Sound, and sea passageways such as the Northeast Providence Channel. Cuba and the other Antilles would be much larger and some of the islands would be connected by land where now only the tips of submerged mountains break the surface. Florida would extend east into the Atlantic and in the west far into the Gulf of Mexico. The eastern seaboard from Florida to Long Island would extend seventy-five to a hundred miles farther into the ocean than it does today, with the Hudson River cutting through gigantic canyons, which are now submerged, on its way out to sea. Further

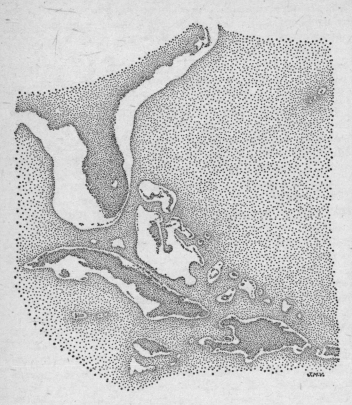

3. *White area off the coast of the continental United States,
the Bahamas, and Antilles indicates what was land approximately twelve thousand years ago before the melting of the
third glaciation raised the sea level and immersed it. What
appears to be man-made constructions on the Bahama Banks
suggests that this land was formerly inhabited by people pos-
sessing a considerable degree of civilization.*

out Bermuda would be a great island with its present banks and some of its sea mounts above the surface, with its shoreline running along the present Bermuda Rise. Farther to the south on the European-African side of the Atlantic the present Madeira and Canary Islands would appear vastly greater than their present size with the Canaries possibly connected to the coast of Africa, while more toward the middle the now relatively small land areas represented by the Azores, a series of large islands and bays covering an area larger than Japan would be located on the Azores plateau along the North Atlantic Ridge. Between the Azores and the Bahamas and extending north of Bermuda lies the Sargasso Sea, a strange stationary sea within the ocean, characterized by floating seaweed, the sargassum, throughout its area. This seaweed is perhaps descended from earth-growing plant life which, when the land sank beneath the sea, adapted and continued to grow.

The theory of an Atlantean Empire having existed in the Atlantic Ocean is based on the assumption that many areas now underwater were once land and also, vice versa, as in the case of the Sahara, whose sea shells and other remains of marine life point out that it was once sea bottom. But legends and traditions to the contrary, the supposition that humanity once developed a seafaring empire on the then larger islands and archipelagoes of the Atlantic whose waters may now cover its sunken cities, temples, golden-roofed palaces, harbors, and great walls, remains a theory until some vestige of these constructions or ruins of them can be located.

Historians and archaeologists are understandably unwilling to consider the onetime existence of Atlantis as a possibility, and consequently the Atlantis legend itself has fallen into a gulf of scholarly disbelief, and proponents of the theory are usually considered eccentrics or visionaries. One can perhaps sympathize with this point of view inasmuch as *if* the factual existence of a worldwide sea power such as Atlantis were established, then history would have to be rewritten and the beginnings of civilization would have to be pushed back in time thousands of years before the earliest cultures such as those of the Egyptians, Sumerians, Babylonians, and the early Mediterranean seagoing peoples.

As if in support of the scholarly scientific viewpoint, years of Atlantean research have revealed, until very recently, no tangible ruins beneath the Atlantic other than cities, walls, and roads in the greenish or purplish depths, sighted from planes or even from fishing boats. These were usually reported as having been seen under special conditions when the water was abnormally clear, but later could not be found again. Some of these reports were put down to the imagination of pilots or to the reticence of fishermen to tell of what they had observed, especially in coastal waters. On some of the Atlantic islands and on the eastern coast of the Americas, ruins have been found which did not fit the local cultural patterns, but these were generally ascribed to the ancient Phoenicians (who kept their Atlantic voyages secret under threat of death) or other pre-Columbian explorers.

Dr Maurice Ewing, the noted oceanographer, expressed his opinion of Atlantis in terms of his own experience having 'spent 13 years exploring the Mid Atlantic Ridge [and] found no trace of sunken cities,' apparently concluding that if he could not find them they did not exist. Two other prehistorians and writers on Atlantis, Armando Vivante and J. Imbelloni, of Argentina, spent a number of years researching the subject and concluded not only that Atlantis never existed but that the study of it was a waste of time. Whether they concluded that the time they spent on *their* books was time wasted has not been specified.

Within the last few years, however, developments have taken place that may be the first steps in establishing the authenticity of the Atlantis legend, whether or not this is pleasing to the scientific community or whether or not it upsets the neatly arranged tables dealing with the dates and cultures of ancient history. This information has come from an eminently logical place to look for Atlantis – the underwater banks and gulfs of the Bermuda Triangle.

Underwater ruins, apparently vestiges of stone platforms, roads, walls, and buildings, were first noted off the coasts of Bimini and Andros in 1968, sometimes first sighted from the air and then verified by divers or sometimes even first seen on the clear sea bottom from surface craft. It is possible, of course, that fishermen and local divers had seen these ruins before and maintained a discreet silence because of the possibility of treasure, either in the form of archaeological artifacts or gold. It is more probable, however, that storms and seismic shifts in the ocean bottom have uncovered some of these ruins, a development coinciding, oddly enough, with the prediction made twenty-eight years prior to the event by Edgar Cayce, the clairvoyant, many of whose trance-like readings concerned Atlantis. In 1940 Cayce said: 'Poseidia will be among the first portions of Atlantis to rise again – expect it in '68 – '69 – not so far away.'

The circumstances of the discovery of the undersea Bimini Wall (or causeway) by oceanographers Dr Manson Valentine, Dimitri Rebikoff, Jacques Mayol, and others, and the discovery from the air by pilots Trig Adams and Bob Brush of the first of the Andros 'temples,' have been described in detail in several books (including *Mysteries from Forgotten Worlds* – Doubleday, 1972). These first discoveries were almost immediately discounted by archaeologists and oceanographers. The Andros temple and others in the vicinity were considered to be 'lobster crawls' or rectangles built for the collection of conches or sponges, although they were rather meticulously constructed of stones. The Bimini Wall was reported to be a natural break-off of beach rock, resembling a road or platform only to the imaginative.

Since the first negative reaction of established archaeology to the underwater Bahama discoveries, a number of private and institutional expeditions and also various film companies, drawn by the furor over the Triangle, have made underwater inspections and films in the area. In doing so

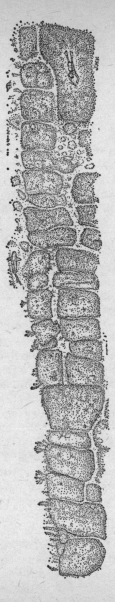

4. Sketch of section of Bimini wall or road indicating size of rocks by figures of man and shark swimming at bottom at approximately twenty-five to thirty feet below surface.

they have verified the existence of a considerable number of other examples of what seem and in some cases have proved to be underwater roads, cyclopean walls, tiled stone floors, truncated pyramids, causeways, concentric circles of giant stones, and even stone heads, carved pillars, and statuary, at different points on the sea bottom in the Bahamas, especially off Bimini, Andros, Exuma, Caicos, and Cat Cays. Statuary had reportedly been brought up from the sea bottom in the Bermuda Islands where pilots of submersibles allegedly have seen underwater cities as well. Ruins have been sighted near the Canary and Azores Islands, off the coasts of North Africa and Spain, the north coast of Cuba, and the continental shelf of the United States, and underwater causeways and giant walls off the coasts of Yucatán and Venezuela (cf. *The Mystery of Atlantis* – Avon, 1975). The depths at which these ruins have been located vary from thirty feet to a mile and a half.

In the Bahamas, where the majority of these ruins have been found, perhaps because so many people are looking for them, the depths on the Bahama Banks also vary greatly. Underwater roads near Caicos seem to come out of the depths and run over the shallows and part of the island. The Bimini Wall varies in depth from twenty-five to thirty-five feet, along its thousand-yard (visible) course. A labyrinthine series of walls or chambers about ninety feet deep have been photographed from the air near North Bimini. Far out from shore in two hundred to three hundred feet again at five hundred feet of water large pyramids have allegedly been seen by pilots and visited by divers, the latter taking a somewhat reluctant attitude toward revealing the location of their finds.

This reluctance stems from what we may call submarine archaeological fever – keeping a find secret – so that only the divers themselves can locate and exploit the find or treasure, perhaps even dynamiting the ruins to hasten recovery. Fortunately the Government of the Bahamas has taken steps to protect the underwater finds and a museum has been established at Freeport for the collection of such artifacts that can be taken from the sea bottom and moved to the surface.

Only within the last year or so has firm proof been offered that these unusual walls and ruins are not just rock formations that resemble ancient ruins and that the artifacts on the sea bottom are not 'intrusive,' that is, dropped in an ancient shipwreck. In a series of expeditions (Poseidia 1 and 2) made by Dr David Zink of Lamar University, and independent research by Dr M. Valentine, Dr J. Thorne and others, it has been ascertained that the huge stone blocks of the Bimini road are not part of the beach rock and that a fracture in the bottom does not correspond with the orientation of the great rocks of the wall, which are not part of the bottom of the sea but laid on the bottom – some still resting on pillars, a fairly impossible coincidence if it were a natural formation. The numerous other ruins throughout the islands are now being investigated, and, even while this research is going on, more remains of buildings, walls, platforms, and pyramids are being found in increasingly deeper water.

Whether or not Edgar Cayce meant that Atlantis, its golden palaces dripping with seaweed, would appear out of the waters in 1968, his prophecy was nonetheless essentially true, as buildings and artifacts of a drowned civilization *did* appear before an incredulous world in 1968 – and the rediscovery of a sunken world is continuing in exactly the different parts of the Atlantic where Atlantis was supposed by legend to have existed. These ruins cannot be from any culture we know, since the water level of the oceans and seas rose one fifth of a mile thousands of years before our own first records. Therefore, if the Phoenicians, Minoans, Vikings, Irish, or any other known race suspected of having preceded Columbus did build these huge remains in the places where they have been found, they would have had to build them underwater.

Interest in and research on the Bermuda Triangle may have solved the older mystery – did inhabited and civilized lands once exist in the Western Atlantic? Air reconnaissance over parts of the Atlantic Ocean where the sea bottom can be seen from high altitudes, permitting the concept of an underwater complex to be clearly perceived, indicate that more ruins and perhaps the remains of entire cities on the banks and slopes of the continental shelf of the Atlantic await closer inspection by submarines, specially constructed submersibles, and eventually divers. Changes in pattern of bottom cover have demonstrated that remains of prehistoric buildings, although covered by sand and sea grass, still leave ghostly but clear outlines whose rectangular or circular shapes show that the remains of building complexes are buried not only under the sea but under the sea bottom as well. If a civilization in the Western Atlantic were overwhelmed by a cataclysm of global proportions, its cities would be in ruins and many of the ruins would have sunk into or be covered by the sea bottom in 11,500 years, especially so if volcanic activity had continued in the area ever since, as now seems to have been the case.

Although it is scientifically true that the oceans rose dramatically during the past twelve thousand years to a level sufficient to cover the huge areas where these underwater ruins have been found, we have no clear idea of what happened to Atlantis except that it was covered by the sea. Did it sink 'in a single day and night' in 'violent earthquakes and floods' as reported by Plato? Did the civilization of the world before the Flood cause its own destruction by tampering with the forces of nature? Did a prehistoric atomic war, described in such curious detail in the ancient Hindu epic the *Mahabharata*, contribute to the melting of the glaciers and the flooding of the earth? Even a collision of the earth with a planetoid in the southern area of the Bermuda Triangle has been predicated, and the late Otto Muck, author of *Atlantis – Gefunden* ('Atlantis Found' – Stuttgart, 1954), believed, perhaps with a certain over-enthusiasm, that his research on the Maya calendar indicated that the equivalent date in our calendar of such a collision was June 5, 8498 B.C.

Just as research on the sea bottom of the Bermuda Triangle has uncovered vestiges of what we may term prehistoric Atlantean civilization, investigations of the sinking of Atlantean lands may bring us closer to an explanation of what is happening now in the Bermuda Triangle. The

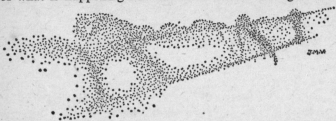

5. *Traces of structures or walls seen from plane at thirty-six thousand feet on sea bottom of Great Bahama Bank west of Andros. Vestiges of construction continue for several miles.*

seismic, tidal, or perhaps cosmic forces that overwhelmed the once populated lands now under the sea may still be at work after thousands of years. The Caribbean and the contiguous portion of the Western Atlantic comprise one of the world's most active volcanic zones and one especially characterized by the sudden and violent sea cyclones whose very name, 'hurricane,' comes from Hurikan, a destructive god of the Carib Indians who, in their belief, caused the Great Flood.

An interesting hypothesis about natural forces operating in a supranatural way in the Bermuda Triangle, as well as an attempt to explain logically and specifically the disappearances of planes, ships, passengers, and crews, is offered by Ronald Waddington of Burlington, Canada, a researcher and theorist on the Bermuda Triangle:

My hypothesis is based on the fact that subterranean volcanic eruptions are taking place continuously. It is conceivable that due to the great depths and pressures of the geosynclines under the Atlantic volcanic eruptions different to the kind that created the Pacific atolls are taking place in this area. Fissures may be opening up in these uncharted depths and the fantastic pressure created by the hot gasses of the earth's core may be expelling chunks of radio-active densely magnetic material unlike anything known to man. This material would move with tremendous velocity, similar to a liquid-fueled rocket. When it broke the surface of the water, like a polaris missile, it might act like a powerful cosmic ray in its attempts to change its electron balance.

The effect of these rays on any plane that came within its magnetic field could short-circuit all electrical equipment. As the ignition system cut out, the plane would instantly lose all lift and plunge into a glide over which the pilot would have no control, as all electrical assists to the controls would also be dead. This instantaneous power shut-off would also explain why no pilot was ever able to send out an S.O.S. even though some were in direct contact with ground controllers. The assumed explosions of planes in the air could be explained by the arcing of shorted electrical circuits igniting the gas vapors as they hit the magnetic field.

The effect of this phenomena on ships would be quite different. Chunks of this radio-active material could shoot to the surface with the velocity of a hydrogen bomb and home-in on the steel hulls of ships like the magnetic head of a torpedo, and with the same devastating results. It is conceivable that a ship hit with such atomic force could disintegrate completely, which explains why no survivors or floating wreckage is found.

The peculiar phenomena of the ships that have been found afloat with no one aboard ... can be explained by assuming that these eruptions, like all known volcanic eruptions, vary in magnitude and duration. These ships may have been bombarded with smaller fragments not powerful enough to sink the ship. The terrifying spectacle of these fire-bombs suddenly emerging from the sea and bombarding the ship would throw the crew into such a panic that they would immediately abandon ship. The boiling turbulence of the water, usually associated with a subterranean volcanic eruption, coupled with the panic-stricken actions of the crew would preclude any hope of survivors from such a disaster.

The remarks of the few radio operators who were able to describe what they saw before their sets went dead make no sense whatever, until you relate them to the fire-balls and water turbulence that a subterranean disturbance of this kind might create, then they make very good sense indeed and are perfectly logical.

The fact that these mysterious happenings only take place on certain dates, and that thousands of ships and planes pass through this busy area without incident seems to indicate that these incidents have a cyclic characteristic similar to volcanos.

These kinds of peculiar eruptions could of course be taking place in other areas, such as the vast Pacific, a long way from busy shipping lanes and air lanes. Perhaps some of the mysterious disappearances around Japan and other areas of the Pacific could be looked into more closely to see if they fit into the pattern of deep geosynclines and subterranean ridges ...

While Waddington's suggestions predicate no link between Atlantis and the present occurrences in the Bermuda Triangle, the series of reactions he describes might, nevertheless, have endured to this day as a by-product of the catastrophe that caused the Atlantean lands to sink beneath the ocean.

The onetime existence of Atlantis and the present day existence of the Bermuda Triangle are two of the ocean's outstanding mysteries. The explanation of one may lead to the solution of the other.

There are indications, however, that the occurrences in the Bermuda Triangle cannot be categorized solely as coming from volcanic disturbances below and a turbulent sea above. Many other puzzling factors must also be considered. These include the unusual behavior of clouds, the sudden appearance of glowing fogs, 'whiteouts' accompanied by electromagnetic malfunction, unidentified lights or craft moving in and out of vision through the night sky or below the surface of the sea, or from under the sea to the sky and back again, and finally 'phantom' radar sightings of objects on the radar screen that apparently have no material form.

The suggestion has been made that these phenomena too may be linked to former or even present Atlantean activity in the area, and the theory exists, based largely on Edgar Cayce's references to Atlantean power sources – that sunken power complexes may still be in a state of sporadic operation even after thousands of years under the sea. But whatever may be the cause of these occurrences, whether of seismic, electromagnetic, or human or alien origin, they are increasingly a source of surprise and bewilderment to travellers through the area who encounter these forces – that is, to those who survive them.

CHAPTER SIX

REPORTS FROM THE EDGE OF REALITY

Pilots, passengers, yachtsmen, fishermen, and seamen within the Bermuda Triangle are no longer as reticent as they formerly were to recount their observations and experiences within the area, however unusual and frequently unrelated they may be. This new manifestation naturally does not yet apply to the agencies and organizations who understandably, from the point of view of self-interest or protection, encourage the impression that there is nothing really unusual happening in the Bermuda Triangle and that the long list of recurring disappearances is somehow normal. Meanwhile people, planes, and ships continue to vanish without trace as before. There now exist considerably more numerous descriptions of circumstances which have been encountered by other individuals, who did *not* vanish and lived to report some of the attendant phenomena which may have been the last view of life (as we know it) for others who did not survive to tell about it. These accounts may represent reports from the edge of disaster – from the fringe of the area of aberration – in other words, not well enough inside it to bring their observations, as well as their lives, to a definite conclusion.

A Cessna 172, piloted by Mike Roxby and carrying two passengers, Don Parris and Kelly Hanson, flying to Haiti on December 16, 1974, encountered a variety of aberrations and finally met its doom while apparently pursued by a swirling cloud which 'appeared from nowhere' and caused them to crash into a hill on Great Inagua, killing the pilot but only injuring the passengers. As reported in the Florida press, instrument malfunction began when the small plane had passed Bimini. The four radios on board suffered blackouts and the plane's navigation instruments as well as the fuel gauge ceased to operate. The pilot, navigating by the sun, although unable to locate familiar landmarks, had made a landing on an open area between sugar cane fields but had left rather hurriedly after a few words exchanged with several of the local inhabitants indicated that he was in Cuba. Airborne again, he made radio contact with another plane and established a course to Great Inagua in the Bahamas, but then the radio blacked out again. As the plane was coming in for a landing, Hanson said, 'One second everything was clear and we could see the airstrip perfectly. Then we were suddenly in the middle of a swirling cloud that just appeared from nowhere.' The pilot was killed in the resulting crash, the airport manager later stating: 'He was an experienced pilot. There seems to be no obvious explanation for the crash.' Don Parris, one of the surviving passengers, made a further observation: 'You have heard about the Devil's Triangle – you see movies about it – but you can't believe it, really. Well, I believe it now.'

While natural clouds are not likely to pursue, swallow up, or disintegrate planes by themselves, one cannot nevertheless escape the chilling supposition that sometimes, within what seems to be a 'normal' cloud seen at the time of a well-witnessed loss, there may be contained something – condition, matter, or void – that has contributed to the disappearance of the aircraft or vessel.

It is difficult not to 'suspect' a cloud formation in connection with the disappearance of a U.S.A.F. Super Sabre in an incredible incident which took place in sight of Bermuda in January 1960, witnessed by observers on the ground, in the air, and from surface craft in the adjacent waters.

Victor Haywood, formerly of Bermuda and now living in Wakefield, Yorkshire, England, was an eyewitness to the incident. In 1960 Haywood was employed on the Satellite Tracking Program on which two civilian firms, English Electric of Stafford, England, and Construction Management of New York, were working. Haywood was therefore a daily visitor to the Military Air Base at Kindley Field. Haywood describes the occurrence in his own words:

About 1300 hours on a bright, almost cloudless day, five Super-Sabres (fighters) of the American Air Force took off from the military airbase at Kindley (St Davids), Bermuda. This writer, along with four or five others who worked on the island, watched the take-off with interest because the Super-Sabre was a relatively rare aircraft then – at least insofar as appearances in Bermuda were concerned.

With the assistance of their afterburners the aircraft were soon airborne. They formed up and flew into a large cloud approximately half a mile offshore. The whole of that cloud, at least the two dimensional circumference of it, was entirely visible to us watchers; at the same time the five planes were on shore tracking radar, this being a normal approach and depart procedure laid down by the military authorities.

Five fighters went into the cloud, four emerged on the other side. The radar tracking sets never saw a 'fall' despite the aircrafts' altitude of several hundred feet. We never saw anything fall either! Within minutes the loss of the Super-Sabre was reported and a search instigated almost immediately – it was merely half a mile offshore and the water quite shallow. There was never anything found to indicate a crashed aeroplane except a life-jacket of standard Air Force pattern. This was never seriously considered as belonging to the missing machine because, Bermuda being garrisoned by thousands of military personnel, and many Islanders owning sailing vessels – well, human nature being what it is, scores of Bermudians had Air Force life-jackets which they weren't entitled to have. That piece of merchandise found during the search could have just as easily come from that quarter as any other.

There was never a satisfactory answer as to what happened to that aircraft or the pilot. Needless to say an intensive investigation conducted by the USAF produced no explanation nor shed any light on the mystery.

As has been noted previously, disappearances of planes and unusual incidents that occur to other planes that do not disappear sometimes happen on the same day in the same general area of the Triangle, sometimes at the same altitude level. Jim Blocker, a corporate flight pilot from Atlanta, may owe his survival to a slight modification of his flight plans. His experience occurred in February 1968 in a flight from Nassau to Palm Beach. As Blocker recalls:

The weather was clear and I filed an original flight plan for an altitude of 8,000 feet but the control tower recommended that I change to 6,000 feet because *two other planes* flying at 8,000 feet had disappeared without a trace that same day. About 40 miles north of Nassau my radio went dead, my compass started spinning, and all my navigational aids stopped working, including my very high frequency directional finder – and that's unheard of! When I finally came out of the clouds I was *150 miles northeast of Nassau....* and I had been heading *northwest!*

Some experiences suggest that some kind of electric energy occasionally takes the shape of fireballs that seemingly drive straight to iron ships and, perhaps by extension, to aluminum planes. A report by W. J. Morris, an ex-seaman now living in Llantrisant, South Wales, Great Britain, is illustrative of this phenomenon:

In the summer of 1955 I was serving aboard the motor vessel *Atlantic City*. One morning while approaching Newport News, I was on lookout duty situated on the 'monkey island' atop the wheelhouse.

It was a calm, balmy morning – calm, but with the usual swell. It was dawn, but the sun was not up yet. The ship was on Iron Mike (automatic steering).

The officer of the watch joined me after a while for a chat. All of a sudden he gave out a yell. The ship was going mad, steering a circle.

At that very moment we both saw what seemed to be a ball of fire travelling at great speed at us on what seemed like a collision course. I panicked and went to jump over the wind dodger on to the foredeck.

The mate, sensing what I was about to do, hit me to the deck and threw himself down also. The ball of fire went over us. There was no noise, no roar, but when we got to our feet there was a strange turbulence on the sea.

We dashed down to the wheelhouse. The gyro compass was dead, and the binnacle compass was dancing in its bowl. I took the wheel and under the officer's instructions steadied the ship, bringing her back to course.

The ship's gyro and electrical gear never functioned again during the voyage and had to be repaired in port.

Highly unusual and extremely sudden electronic manifestations, of which the fireball described by Morris perhaps was one, have been vividly described by Wayne Bandora, Petty Officer, Second Class Crewman, on a Navy P2 during a training flight in December 1970 off the east coast of Florida. His account is of special interest because of the instrument failure during the sudden magnetic storm:

The sky had been clear as a bell when suddenly, about 1 A.M. great arcs of lightning branched over the sky. Each tremendous flash lasted for what seemed to be an unusually long time in brilliant shades of green and purple. I clocked some on my watch – each flash lasted for 5 or 6 seconds. After a while the lightning started to slip around in front of us. I told the pilot – then he shifted course. The compass had become frozen and he didn't realize it. We lost all electrical power in the nose section. We could not get any response from the radio. Smoke started coming from the starboard engine – black smoke from a probable oil leak. We shut it down but got back successfully. I've flown in 14 countries but I never saw any lightning like that before. You could smell the burnt ozone in the air.

Wildly explosive and prolonged lightning storms have been noted in the Bermuda Triangle since the time of Columbus, the first known chronicler of the area's supranormal behavior. One recalls that the sudden and violent tempest which caused the loss of a homeward-bound Spanish fleet of over twenty galleons from the island of Hispaniola was described by Columbus as resembling nothing so much as a tremendous sea battle, with prolonged salvos of artillery and the smell of gunpowder in the air.

Unusual electronic disturbances, apparently concentrated in the area, may or may not be the cause of the many fast-moving and often pulsating lights above and below the water that form the subject of increasingly frequent reports, sometimes from people who are still reticent to talk about what they have seen.

In this connection, reports from persons who have previously maintained a firm disbelief in unusual or unexplained phenomena are especially revealing. Jack Strehle, a commercial pilot working part time for Opa-Locka Flight Center in Miami, was concerned, according to some of the other pilots, because of something that had happened on a flight back from Bimini a few days before Christmas in 1974. Jim Richardson, a pilot and observer of unusual happenings in the area, several times asked Strehle to tell him what he had seen, but Strehle would say, 'I don't want to talk about it.' Although the pilot in question was reputed to be 'square as a bear' in his unwillingness to accept the unexplainable and 'as big an agnostic as you can find ... he also works for General Electric' (this last observation probably being meant as a recommendation for his cool and level-headed attitude toward the supernatural), Richardson continued his attempts to find out what had happened. Strehle finally told him that on the night in question, about a thousand feet past the north shoreline of Bimini near the Moselle Reef, he suddenly saw a flashing blue light off the right wing of his plane. Then, obtaining a better view, he noted that the object seemed to be round or ellipsoid. As he looked he checked his magnetic compass and saw that it was spinning. Richardson asked, 'How long did you keep the object in sight?' to which the previous skeptic replied, 'Not very long – I just wanted to get the hell out of there.' – a sentiment often shared by pilots, skeptical or nonskeptical, who have found themselves in similar situations.

Another recent convert to acceptance of UFOs in the Bermuda Triangle is Dr Jim Thorne, an oceanographer and scientist with long experience of the sea and the skies above it. Dr Thorne has long maintained a firm opinion that unusual reports from the area, however numerous or well documented they may be, have nevertheless a natural explanation. In the summer of 1975, Dr Thorne was in charge, on board a seventy-foot schooner called the *New Freedom*, of an investigative expedition through the Bermuda Triangle. On the way home from dinner on the island of Bimini, on the night of August 2, he and another diver were walking along the beach when suddenly, in the starlit sky:

> A single star seemed to detach itself from the others and come straight towards us. It hovered directly above us and then moved to the right. It maneuvered first to the right, then to the left, and back again. It appeared to stop dead in the sky and hover over different parts of the entire island and the sea around it. I would calculate its speed at several thousand miles per hour. It seemed to be a bluish white — and also to vibrate. At times we thought we heard a buzzing sound or, rather, a steady oscillation of sound. We observed it for a full three and a half minutes. It was close enough for us to see its shape. When it got close I saw it was lighted with blue-lights. It started away very fast.
>
> I've always been very pragmatic [about UFOs] — never believed in them. I'm convinced about what I saw. I'm not saying it was extraterrestrial but it *was* a UFO, that is, it was certainly unidentified. Walt Henrick, one of the divers, was with me, a rather unemotional guy. His comment was: 'I've seen it but I don't believe it.'

While there still seems to be a certain reticence among pilots, sea captains, and other observers acting in the course of duty to report UFOs, they are sometimes less reticent to discuss other unusual occurrences in the Bermuda Triangle, especially if the incident seems to relate to natural phenomena and is not connected with officially unacceptable UFOs.

Bob Brush, commercial pilot on a night flight over the Bahamas, aboard a DC-6 cargo plane in August 1974, was startled by a sudden all-encompassing bright light which so lit up the surrounding area with its brilliance that he could clearly observe the ground of the nearby islands of Providence, Watlings, and North Caicos as well as the surface of the sea. According to his account, his eyes hurt from the brilliance, which was sustained for a number of seconds, and he clearly remembered that, although the whole area was illuminated to an estimated 4,000 Kelvin light rating, it seemed to be the 'wrong kind of light' and 'there were no shadows.'

Electromagnetic manifestations characterized by bolts of fire, sustained lightning, or other sources of light, indicative as they are of the forces present and unpredictably active in the area of the Bermuda Triangle, do not, however, explain the sudden and unexplained behavior of a calm surface sea, frequently noted by sailors and aircraft pilots. One of these phenomena concerns 'holes' or trenches within the surface of the sea itself, which evidently were not whirlpools or the result of waves, while another describes a field of water, not waterspouts, mushrooming in a single mass over the surface of the sea. This phenomenon, a huge raised level of the sea about half a mile high, may be what was witnessed by the pilots of a Boeing 707 on April 11, 1963, and reported at 19°54' north latitude, 66°47' west longitude.

A rather convincing account of an experience with holes or gulleys in the surface of the sea is recounted by Irwin Brown, fisherman and boat skipper. The incident took place in the vicinity of Long Key – north of Key West, Florida, in the early part of May 1965.

My wife and I were on our way back from a fishing trip – we had a 135 HP Evinrude Cobra – the same boat conservation men use – about 25 miles from shore south east from Long Key, about 15 miles from Tennessee Light. It was a beautiful day and the water was absolutely calm. I had just made a complete 360° inspection to the horizon and remarked to my wife: 'There's absolutely nothing around us – just you and me.' The water was extremely clear. I could see fish down to about 50 feet – we were in perhaps 1500 to 2000 feet of water.

We were doing about 35 knots. I was looking ahead and suddenly saw a trench in the sea about 4 feet deep and 20 feet wide. It looked like it had been made by a bulldozer. There was no turbulence of the sea – like the wake of a boat. It went dead right and left to our course. I'm in the construction business and it struck me that it looked the same as if a bulldozer had ploughed a square trench through earth – except that this was through water. As I looked at it the boat lurched out from under me – I pitched forward and landed on my wrist. I cut off the engine and tried to help my wife. I picked her up off the deck, and we later found she had broken two ribs. I looked back for the trench but we had drifted past the spot. We talked to people about it when we got to shore but no one could explain it. Somebody said it might have been the wake of a submarine, but it was no wake, the trench was too square.

Besides trenches or holes which suddenly seem to open in the ocean, fountains of water, which are not weather-connected waterspouts, are occasionally noted. These may be the results of underwater seismic explosions (although such activity should affect a larger area) or perhaps controlled explosions from torpedoes or tests from submarines.

A former member of the crew of the *Queen Mary*, equipment supervisor Ray Clarke, observed a peculiar fountain of water rising from an area in the eastern section of the Triangle in the late afternoon of a day in September 1954:

... I was employed aboard the Queen Mary, about September in 1954, on an Eastward crossing from New York ... I happened to be looking astern one early evening, time about 5 P.M., and noticed an area of the sea gradually turning from a darkish green color to a very pale apple green color and it looked very much as if that area was becoming flat and calm. Quite suddenly a column of water shot up, what I would estimate at being approximately 15 to 25 feet wide and rising to about 50 feet in height. This was followed by a similar column about half a mile apart from the first and both momentarily continued, with the second column finishing before the first. The sea then seemed to go back to normal in color. At that time there did not seem to be any other ship in the vicinity that could be seen, and I did report the matter to an Officer of the watch ...

Such sudden undersea fountains appearing without warning in calm weather could cause yachts and other small surface craft to founder. An unexpected rush of water may have caused the loss of the *Drosia*, a recent victim of the Triangle. The *Drosia*, a 315-foot Liberian freighter, sailing with a cargo of sugar in good weather off Cape Hatteras on the morning of December 11, 1975, at about 4 A.M., sank so suddenly that there was no time to send an SOS. The captain, who was saved with more than half of the crew, reported that the ocean was a little choppy, but offered no explanation about why the big ship broke up and sank in less than four minutes.

Powerful waves, referred to as seiche waves in oceanography and forming hundreds or thousands of miles away, sometimes appear in a calm sea to the detriment of surface craft. It has been suggested that this happened to the U.S.S. *Cyclops* (No. 30 in map in the illustrated section) as well as other vessels in the past. But if this had been the cause of the loss of the *Drosia*, other ships would also have noted the giant wave.

Undersea volcanic explosions also have been suspected of causing the disappearances of other vessels, the *Freya* (No. 11 on the map), and the *Kaiyo Maru No. 5*, the Japanese research ship that vanished in the Japanese counterpart of the Bermuda Triangle, the Devil Sea, in 1955. However, in the recent case of the *Drosia*, neither of these elements was noted, and the possibility exists that the *Drosia* was hit or torn apart by an object or force from *below* it. The fact that there were survivors was of no help in establishing what had happened, as they were not able to advance any explanation. It is probable that with the focus of public attention on the happenings within the Triangle, accounts of survivors from sudden and unexplained sinkings may provide a link between the observance of unusual phenomena and the loss or near loss of a nearby (or one's own) vessel or aircraft.

The hazy light which sometimes suddenly appears during calm seas and clear weather may be a reason for the frequent and persistent mirages reported in the Triangle by people who habitually traverse the area. Strange and unexplainable objects suddenly appear – or familiar objects inexplicably vanish. Under a sunlit and cloudless sky the 281-foot radio mast on South Bimini, the landmark for the harbor entrance, suddenly vanished for an entire hour from the sight of the occupants of a thirty-six-foot sloop who were taking their bearings on it, although, according to the account of Judge Ellis Meacham, of Fort Lauderdale, who was on board the sloop, 'Everything else on shore was plainly visible – the sky cloudless, the sun shining brightly. The radio mast had become invisible, but trees, houses, boats, etc. were still clearly visible in the area where we were last watching the mast with its red lights blinking "B" three times a minute.' Not until they followed a boat into the harbor were they able to see the mast again. Incidentally, it had remained visible to other boats not in their immediate area.

This fogginess on a sunlit day has been reported by numerous ship captains and yachtsmen. It frequently occurs at a time when radio communication is interrupted. Joe Talley encountered this phenomenon several times while on shark fishing expeditions between Key West and Tortuga. He expressed it as 'clear around the boat – clear for miles – but for some reason there was no horizon. You couldn't see a line on the horizon, nothing but whiteness.' On another occasion, in 1944, Joe Talley was the sole survivor of his boat, the *Wild Goose*, which, while in tow, was seen by the crew of the towboat to be suddenly covered by an encompassing mist, completely covering the *Wild Goose*, which pulled so hard on the towline that the captain of the towboat, about to be drawn into the fog, cut the cable. The *Wild Goose* never came out of the fog, although Joe Talley, the lone survivor, did, after suffering a prolonged underwater ascent following a towline at an estimated fifty to eighty feet below the surface. The *Wild Goose*, with its four occupants, was never found, with no indication as to whether it had been pulled into the depths or had somehow disintegrated.

The fog which suddenly covered the boat in tow by the *Good News*, in 1966, in the Tongue of the Ocean, as reported by Captain Don Henry and his crew (described in *The Bermuda Triangle*), was also a localized thick fog or mist covering apparently only a small area, that of the boat in tow, almost as if it were part of a 'smoke screen' operation. It is interesting to remember that while the boat in tow was completely covered by the mist and the towboat was not, nevertheless a complete power cutoff was noted on all electric appliances and outlets on the towboat, as if the power drain extended some distance beyond the mysterious fog.

The many reported instances of fast-moving lights in the sky or below the surface of the sea, sudden fogs which appear to move toward and encompass ships and planes as if they were targets, and unusual behavior of a certain patch of sea, seem to occur in an impersonal, haphazard manner, with no immediate effect on those who see them until it is too late to take evasive action, as in the case of Captain Talley and others, who have flown or sailed into fogs from which they never emerged. Sometimes, however, these unusual sightings in the Triangle tend to affect the observers directly, even menacing their surface craft, and some potential victims have survived and have been able to report their encounters. Don Delmonico, from Miami, a lifelong sailor and owner of cargo boats, experienced two surprise encounters with unidentified submarine objects, once in August 1969, and again in October, while fishing for lobsters around Great Isaac Island, Bahamas. Delmonico was at the bow of his thirty-foot boat when, to his understandable consternation, he suddenly saw, clearly visible in the almost transparent waters of the Bahamas, at a depth of about twelve feet, a gray elliptical object over a hundred feet long, rushing toward him at an estimated speed of seventy miles per hour. He noted that the course of his boat was about forty-five degrees toward the Gulf Stream, but the object, whatever it was, was moving along the path of the Gulf Stream. As the object approached him, for what appeared to be a final confrontation, it suddenly veered to port, leaving his ship intact to sail another day and even to have a second encounter with the same or similar craft.

He had not long to wait. Two months later, in October, on board his boat in the vicinity of Great Isaac Light on a collision course with another (or the same) unidentified submarine object and, because of its proximity, obtained an even closer view. According to his recollection it was light gray, about the same size as the one he had previously seen, with no ports, no fins, no superstructure, and no evi-dent propellers, moving seemingly by some other means of propulsion. It appeared to be between 150 and 200 feet long, much too large to be a torpedo.

His second escape seemed to him to be even closer than the first. The somewhat shallower depth of maneuver on the island side in the area where he found himself and the great speed of the object seemed to be bringing it directly toward his boat, so quickly that he was unable to get out of its path. In his words he 'cut the motor and just prayed' as, to his surprise, the metallic-appearing object 'ducked under the boat' and continued on its way to vanish in the blue distance.

Descriptions of these unidentified submarine objects from pilots who have tracked them from the air over the Bermuda Banks tally with that given by Don Delmonico, as well as one encountered by the PX-15 *Ben Franklin*, a submarine especially equipped for prolonged underwater research, drifting through the area under the direction of

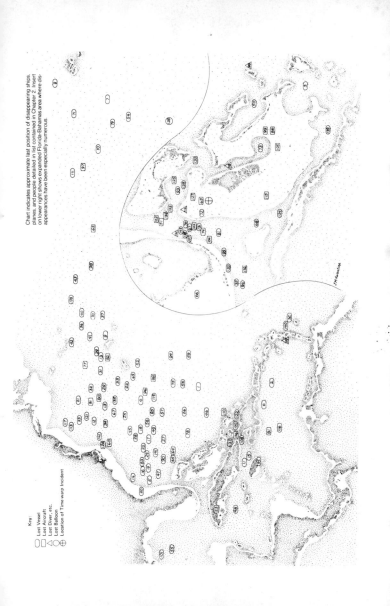

Chart indicates approximate last position of disappearing ships, planes, and people detailed in list contained in Chapter 2. Insert on lower right shows expanded Florida-Bahamas area where disappearances have been especially numerous.

Key:

Lost Vessel
Lost Aircraft
Lost Diver, etc.
Lost Balloon
Location of Time-warp Incident

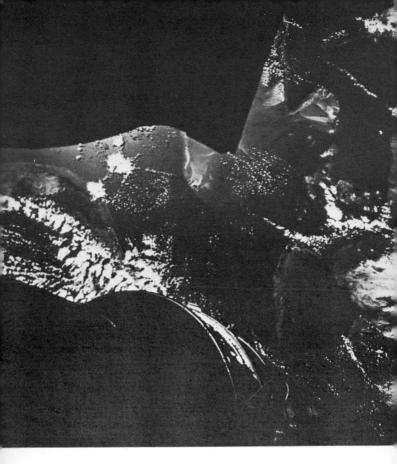

View of western end of Bermuda Triangle. Photo was taken from satellite in orbit. Dark material on upper and lower left is part of satellite's bay opening. Land mass at left, between openings of satellite's bay is the end of Florida, with Gulf Stream flowing northward between Florida and the Great Bahama Bank, shown as submerged area in centre of photo with Bimini located on the left near the drop-off. Other light-coloured area in the lower right is another submerged section of the Great Bahama Bank. Triangular indentation of lower left is the northern area of the Tongue of the Ocean with part of Andros Island to the right. Submerged area in upper right is the Little Bahama Bank on which Abaco and Grand Bahama are located. (Photo: *Courtesy National Aeronautics and Space Administration*).

Above   White water seen from plane at thirty thousand feet over Old Bahama Channel. This white water is a frequently noted and puzzling phenomenon in this area near the Bahamas. (Photo: *Courtesy J M Valentine*).

Below   White glowing water photograph from plane at night near Andros, Bahamas. Pilot Jim Richardson recently landed on white water, collected some, and had it analyzed, with results indicating that it had special chemical properties and a high concentration of sulphur, also traces of strontium and lithium. Although this white water has been variously attributed to stirred-up marl or to banks of fish or smaller marine life, there exists the possibility that it is coming out of crevasses in the sea floor and is a result of volcanic activity. (Photo: *Courtesy J M Valentine*).

Above Wayne Meshejian, a physicist at Longwood College, Virginia, who has made a study of weather satellite communications, has noted that tape relay systems often malfunction over the Bermuda Triangle area. (Photo: *Courtesy Wayne Meshejian*).

Opposite 'Ship wanted' poster as seen on docks in ports and marinas in Florida, the Bahamas, and other islands. It has been theorized that some ships and planes that have reportedly disappeared may have been hijacked, repainted and their appearance otherwise changed. In the case of larger vessels, however, this would be unlikely and sooner or later the story would be uncovered. There were over six hundred craft reported missing without trace off the United States coasts during the two-year period ending in 1976, many of which disappeared within the Triangle. (Photo: *Courtesy Dick Winer*).

Above   The earth as seen from space by Apollo 12. Lower California and the coast of Mexico can be observed slightly above the centre. Following a line from Lower California across Mexico 'at two o'clock', the Gulf of Mexico and Florida can be seen. It is interesting to note that the underwater Bahama Banks can be identified off Florida even at this altitude. (Photo: *Courtesy NASA*).

Right   The S S *Andrew Furuseth* at launching. It was thought that it was from the deck of this ship that several observers noted the sudden disappearance of the D-173 during the course of the Philadelphia Experiment. (Photo: *Courtesy SITU – Society for the Investigation of the Unexplained*).

Above Officers and crew of the S S *Andrew Furuseth* together with visiting officials. It is the opinion of some researchers that the man directly to the left of the ventilator on which the man in the gray suit is sitting may be Carl Allen (or Carlos Allende), who conducted the correspondence with Dr Jessup. (Photo: *Courtesy SITU*).

Right Semiofficial U S Coast Guard photo of UFO taken in 1952 from base in Salem, Massachusetts. 'Semiofficial' is qualified by the fact that this photo has been publicly released by the Coast Guard without definite comments as to what the series of objects were. The photograph was taken in a considerable hurry by Shell Alpert, a corpsman on the base who saw the objects while looking out of a window, ran to get his camera, and took a picture from inside a screen door, showing a series of rapidly travelling luminous objects. Of the thousands of UFOs photographed none of the authenticated ones are particularly clear, principally because of the unexpected nature of their appearances. (Photo: *Courtesy US Coast Guard*).

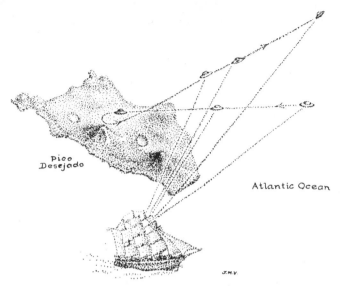

Above Among the thousands of photographs taken of UFOs perhaps the most authenticated picture was taken from the Brazilian Navy Training Ship *Almirante Saldanha* on January 16, 1958, at the island of Trinidade (29° 20′ west longitude, 30° 30′ south latitude) in the South Atlantic. UFOs had been sighted over Trinidade at various times from December 1957 through early 1958. On January 11 personnel on board the *Almirante Saldanha* took photographs of a UFO as it came over the sea from the east, flew up to a mountain on Trinidade along the lines indicated, and returned eastward again over the ocean until lost to sight. (Source of photo: *Brazilian Navy*).

Left View of the UFO approaching coast of Trinidade from the deck of the *Almirante Saldanha*. (Source of photo: *Brazilian Navy*).

Left Underwater photograph of the Bimini Road, wall, foundation, or pier, showing alignment of huge stone blocks on the sea bottom. The Bimini Road was the first definite archaeological find to be made on the Bahama Banks, and its authenticity as an artifact, although previously doubted, has been reinforced by subsequent finds. (Photo: *Courtesy J M Valentine*).

Below Stone slab taken from underwater construction now in Bahama Antiquities Institute. Fossilized mangrove roots growing *over* the stone have been carbon dated from six thousand to eight thousand years before the present era. (Photo: *Courtesy J M Valentine*).

Some of the stones on the sea floor in the Bimini area are resting on other stones and, on some occasions, are supported by small pillars – a rather conclusive indication of their having been part of a building complex. (Photo: *Courtesy J M Valentine*).

Dr J Manson Valentine preparatory to making a surface dive on underwater stone foundations. Dr Valentine, together with Jacques Mayol and Harold Climo, discovered the Bimini Road in 1968, the same year in which, by an almost incredible coincidence, Edgar Cayce had prophesied that parts of Atlantis would begin to be rediscovered. Cayce's prophecy was made in 1940, decades before any underwater ruins were suspected to be on the Bahama Banks. (Photo: *Courtesy J M Valentine*).

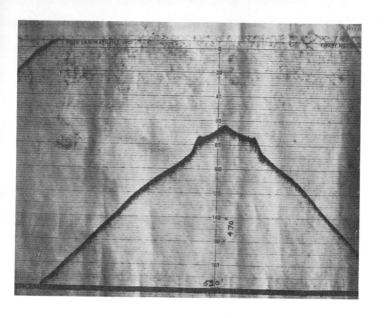

Side-scanning or fish-finding sonar has indicated large masses on sea bottom which suggest pyramids and other buildings. This profile obtained by Captain Don Henry from his fishing boat, equipped with fish-finding sonar, shows what appears to be a pyramid, not on the banks but on the other side of the drop-off. The height is estimated at 420 feet with a base of 540 feet. If this is a pyramid it should compare impressively with the Great Pyramid of Gizeh, Egypt, with a height of somewhat over 480 feet. (Photo: *Courtesy Captain Don Henry and Gene Condon*).

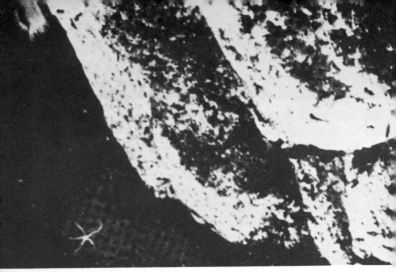

Above An indication of the very deep submergence of former inhabited and civilized areas may have been found off the coast of Peru, in November 1965, when oceanographer Robert Menzies obtained this surprising photograph while taking pictures of bottom fish with a camera lowered from the research ship *Anton Bruun*. The photograph showed the surprising presence of walls or columns standing on an otherwise flat sea bottom at a depth of six thousand feet. Other pictures showed what appeared to be fallen or broken columns implying sudden seismic action and subsidence into the depths perhaps at the time of a like cataclysm in the Western Atlantic. (Photo: *Courtesy Dr Robert J Menzies*).

Opposite above Photograph taken from space of Grand Bahama, Great Abaco (upper part of photo), and the Berry Islands (lower centre). The light colour surrounding the land areas shows banks that were above water from twelve to thirteen thousand years ago before the melting of the third glaciation. Inasmuch as what appear to be man-made structures have been found on other underwater shelves in the Bahamas, it can be expected that future finds will be made on the sunken lands off Great Bahama and Great Abaco as well. (Photo: *Courtesy NASA*).

Opposite below Hexagonal formations on sea bottom near drop-off, Moselle Reef, Bimini. The regular shape of these formations implies that they are man-made, although their purpose whether they are roads, market places, or palace floors, is unknown. (Photo: *Courtesy J M Valentine*).

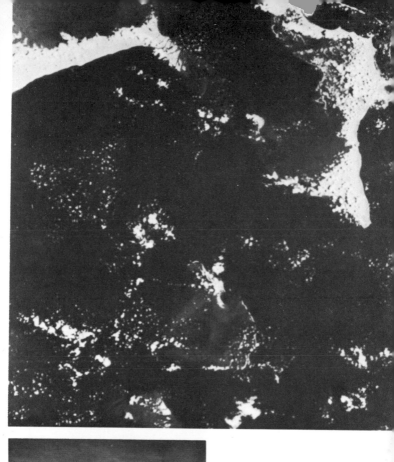

Above Large triple circle of stones on sea bottom off Andros, reminiscent of prehistoric 'calendar' circles or markers, such as those of Stonehenge, Carnac, and South America. Many of the sites of what are apparently ruins of man-made structures have been discovered within the past few years probably as a result of tides or storms uncovering what was previously hidden. Some of the sites, however, have since been again hidden by subsequent storms. (Photo: *Courtesy J M Valentine*).

Left Lines connecting keys south of Andros suggesting that they are vestiges of walls or roads when the outlying keys were once part of a much larger Andros. (Photo: *Courtesy Bob Brush*).

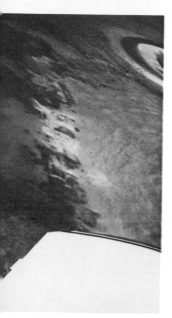

Left Submerged wall or dam photographed from plane off North Bimini. Stones used in construction are of considerable size, comparable to those used in 'Bimini Road'. (Photo: *Courtesy J M Valentine*).

Below Underwater wall, dike or dam shown in top centre of picture taken from greater altitude. Certain features of sea bottom suggest that a larger Bimini may have been used as a port as the waters rose in stages. (Photo: *Courtesy J M Valentine*).

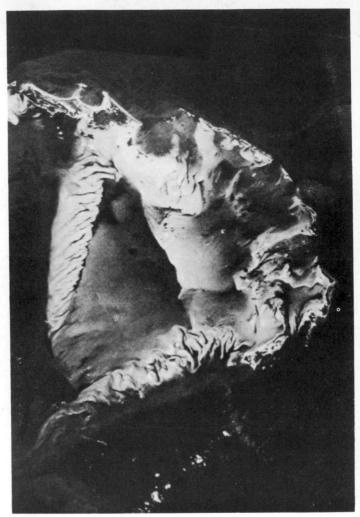

Infrared picture taken from Apollo 16 at an altitude of fifty miles. The infrared film, because of the temperature differentials in the different layers of water, has picked up the bottom contour. The fact that the bottom contour is clearly shown indicates that the bottom is warmer than the covering water. Bits of land area breaking the surface in upper right section of photograph are the Berry Islands. (Photo. *Courtesy NASA*).

Jacques Piccard on a project related to the study of currents, from which were seen several rather unusual objects including a gray-white elliptical object about a hundred feet long going past the *Ben Franklin* at a high rate of speed.

One is inclined to wonder whether these underwater manifestations might possibly be rapid and therefore mistaken viewings of underwater 'clouds' or formations of equally undetermined origin. Submarine clouds or false bottom banks have been observed through the years and have been the subject of numerous reports based on sonar readings of the true bottom of the ocean, which, on occasion, seems to change its reading and thereby vary its previously established depth. This sonar report of a 'false' bottom is usually attributed to banks of fish or smaller marine life.

A large gray-white mass was twice seen by Robert Kuhne, a drawbridge engineer and an occasional fisher for dolphins. Both incidents took place between 11 A.M. and noon in March and May 1975, about 7 miles south and 4 miles east of Fowey Rock, South Carolina, off Key Biscayne, Florida, during the time that he was 'drift fishing' for dolphins. He noticed a clearly defined massive gray-white shape, fairly stationary about fifteen feet below his boat (the bottom was about 230 feet), but he could not catch it on his depth finder as it was apparently out of range and unable to be penetrated by the sonar. It seemed to cover or be hovering over an extensive area much too large to be a hammerhead shark (eighteen to twenty feet) often seen in the vicinity of Fowey Light and locally referred to as a 'freight train.' After the second sighting, with what may be considered the zeal of a true investigator, Kuhne attempted to dive on the object but found on entering underwater that the object was now considerably deeper than his first estimate of fifteen feet. Becoming understandably apprehensive, he then left the water and the area.

One wonders whether this sighting was a USO similar to those seen by shipowner Don Delmonico as well as other shipmasters and pilots. The above case was not fast moving like the others but stationary – whether for making observations or other purposes. Dr Manson Valentine, in assessing this particular case, offers the suggestion that perhaps the gray mass was not a concrete underwater object but a magnetic field forming underwater, of such intense concentration as to cause visible cloud effects on the surrounding water.

Other underwater and luminous cloud formations seem to belong to a different category, of a type that appears to be coming, in the vicinity of the Bahama Banks and in the deep water off the edge of the continental shelf, from crevasses or fissures in the bottom of the sea. They are often referred to as the 'luminous waters' of the Bahamas (although they are occasionally visible off Florida and Cuba, as well), and their luminosity is so strong that they were specifically noted by the first United States astronauts as the last light that they were able to see from the earth. (Columbus' crews saw them as the first light they noticed in the sea as they approached the New World.) They have frequently been ascribed by oceanographers to banks of luminous diatoms, minute organisms called dinoflagellates, or simply marl stirred up from the bottom by banks of fish.

More recent observations of these luminous 'plumes' are convincingly indicative that they are not a fish phenomenon – but something else. For one thing, the shape of the plumes, when seen before they widen and dissolve, resembles smoke coming out of a chimney; tight at the point of egress and spreading thereafter. A recent observation flight off Orange Cay, Bahamas, sighted two distinct parallel plumes of the mysterious luminosity proceeding for some distance before merging in a luminous cloud. A pilot investigator, Jim Richardson, of Miami, landed in his seaplane directly on one of these luminous patches and collected a sample of water from the spot. The water smelled strongly of sulfur and later, when subjected to analysis, indicated a sulfur content up to 20 per cent and precipitated calcite, suggesting the presence of hot, intrusive rocks below the surface. While this escaping underwater

'smoke' may be a completely natural extrusion of substance from the hot interior of the earth, not to be wondered
at, considering the instability of the bottom of the Atlantic,
one is nevertheless reminded of the theory that power
sources from a civilization of prehistory, now lying on the
floor of the Atlantic as a result of sudden changes in the
crust of the earth, may still function periodically or sporadically (and thereby affect the controls and instruments of
modern air and surface craft) despite a hundred intervening
centuries. Another theory, equally unacceptable to the
scientific establishment, would be the existence of present-
day underwater or submarine *and* subterranean power complexes administered by as yet unidentified entities.

It is these that may have been, in the opinion of some
observers, the unidentified underwater craft that have frequently appeared to be on collision course with small craft
operators or that have been observed and clocked by planes
flying over the Bermuda Banks. While, because of their
speed and sudden appearance, these vehicles have not so
far been photographed, a photographic record may have
been made showing traces of their passage along the sea
bottom and perhaps also of their temporary or ultimate
destinations. Straight lines are not found in nature. Dr
Manson Valentine, flying with Pilot Jim Richardson over
the ocean fifteen miles off Chubb Cay on September 5,
1974, observed and followed a pair of completely straight
lines on the sea bottom at a depth of about fifty feet. The
plane followed them for eighteen miles until they appeared
to end at holes of uncertain depth in the bottom of the sea.
The holes were located within a sandy patch different from
the surrounding sea bottom in that no vegetation grew in
this immediate area. Since then Dr Valentine has located
other straight lines on the sea bottom and tracked them in
shallow or deep water *over and across intervening islands*,
the same undeviating lines coming up on land and then
continuing to make a straight path on the ocean floor on
the other side of the island. In the opinion of Dr Valentine
the explanation of these unusual paths does not lie in either

torpedo firings, anchor chains from drifting boats, or the
tracks of underwater currents. Their extremely straight
allineation, narrow width, the fact that they cross over
islands, and their terminals in underwater holes indicate
that they are a phenomenon, like so many of the phenomena present in the Bermuda Triangle, not yet identified
or explained.

A future expedition to be undertaken by Dr Valentine
and his associates will endeavor to ascertain why no grass
grows in the area of these holes, and what may be found
deep within them. This latter aspect will be the responsibility of volunteer divers who will be taken to the spot
by surface craft which, in turn, will be directed toward the
holes by a seaplane.

Divers, 'hard hat,' scuba, and free, have an enviable
opportunity to investigate the sea bottom within the Bermuda Triangle at first hand, an opportunity not always
shared by investigators (or detractors) of the Bermuda Triangle mystery.

Divers have located Spanish galleons from storm-wrecked
or pirate-attacked treasure fleets; they have unexpectedly
found planes and ships, some of which, curiously, were not
even listed as missing, they have discovered cities beneath
the sea, some of which sank in historic times, such as the
'pirate' city of Port Royal, which suddenly sank during an
earthquake in 1692. Within the past several years other
stone cities have been located on the sea bottom off the
Bahamas, whose ancient roads, walls, stone-tiled floors,
foundations, terraces, and pyramids belong to no known
age or culture.

In addition to unsuspected remnants of an unknown
antiquity divers sometimes encounter unnerving examples
of sea life which, although seen in the present, would seem
more correctly to belong to other ages, long past. Some of
these animals, if such they are, have been reported as being
seen close to the surface, unlike the floating 'utility pole,'
which on closer inspection, was noted to have eyes and
flippers as seen by Captain McCamis at a depth of more

than five hundred fathoms (see pages 82–85).

Bruce Mounier, of Miami, an experienced commercial diver and underwater photographer, obtained a good view, while diving in 1968, of what he terms 'an underwater abominable snowman.'

We were south of Great Isaac Light, near the drop-off. I was looking at the bottom while I was being trolled along on a line behind a 30-foot boat built especially for diving and salvage work. I could see a sandy bottom at 35–40 feet. I was deep enough to see ahead of the boat and some sort of round turtle or big fish – about 200 pounds – became visible and I went lower to get a good look. It turned and looked at me at a 20° angle. It had a monkey's face with its head protruding out in front, a much longer neck than a turtle – four or more times the length of a human neck. It rotated its neck like a snake as it watched me. The eyes were like those of a human being, but enlarged. It looked like the face of a monkey with specially adapted eyes for underwater vision. When it got a good look at me it took off – using some form of propulsion that came from underneath.

According to Mounier the creature then made for a cave beneath the overhang of the underwater drop-off, perhaps a fortunate circumstance for Mounier in the light of a Bahamian legend concerning such a monster, called the 'luska,' with a face like an animal's and a neck like a snake's, living in sea caves and feeding off human divers.

Mounier is sure the animal was not a turtle: 'I've caught and sold hundreds of turtles and this was definitely not one. I think it is some unidentified species, it may be a newly developed one, or a very old one we haven't seen before.'

Sometimes unusual fauna are clearly seen in the clear waters or on the surface of the area within the Bermuda Triangle by multiple witnesses whose combined testimonies would seem to contravene the possibility of mass hallucination, especially when the unusual creature encountered is close to the ship in question. The *Santa Clara*, a passenger liner of the Grace Line en route to Cartagena, Colombia, was reported to have run over an unidentified sea monster at 5 P.M. on December 30, 1947. After the incident a radio message was sent to the U.S. Hydrographic Department, as follows:

> LAT 34.34 N LONG 74.07 W 1700 GMT STRUCK MARINE MONSTER KILLING OR BADLY WOUNDING IT PERIOD ESTIMATED LENGTH 45 FEET WITH EEL LIKE HEAD AND BODY APPROXIMATELY THREE FEET IN DIAMETER LAST SEEN THRASHING IN LARGE AREA OF BLOODY WATER AND FOAM SIGHTED BY WM. HUMPHREYS CHIEF OFFICER AND JOHN AXELSON THIRD OFFICER.

As the U.S. Hydrographic Department has the responsibility for marine observation, the captain obviously thought it appropriate to inform the department of the incident as a possible water hazard, although it would perhaps have been of more immediate scientific value to attempt to photograph or retrieve part of the animal for the benefit of the Smithsonian Institution or the Museum of Natural History. In any event the classification of the creature was never established, as it vanished in a wash of blood. It is to be noted that latitude 34° north and longitude 74° west are well within the limits of the Bermuda Triangle.

More recognizable sea creatures, such as giant squids, are credited in certain islands with taking people off fishing boats and even pulling small boats beneath the surface. Captain Joe Talley, a retired shark fisherman (for the commercial use of shark divers) tells of the reticence of local fishermen to stay near the drop-off at night.

> We wanted to set deep water lines off the drop-off at Caicos. But the boys wouldn't stay after sundown. They said that some boats were taken right down by giant squids or something like that. The boats are small, about 25 feet long, and a big thing can crawl aboard very easily. They said that a while ago a giant squid placed a tentacle on the gunnel of a boat and climbed aboard. The boys jumped off and the boat drifted to sea.

Stories and legends of unusual occurrences, monsters – real or imagined – and ghosts have been told in the Bahamas and West Indies for hundreds of years, long before the expression 'Bermuda Triangle' caused a retelling of the old tales and a proliferation of new ones. It is possible that the background or knowledge of legend somehow impels an individual to psychologically create a personal experience. Although this may occur in some cases, it is difficult to believe that this factor alone could have caused Ben Huggard, a champion long-distance swimmer, to imagine the unusual incident he experienced as he accomplished a 162-mile nonstop swim across the open ocean, from Florida to the Bahamas, in May 1975. The physical experience of Ben Huggard, and even his emotional impression while making his cross-Triangle swim, is of considerable interest. Captains, crews, and passengers of planes and ships may have long thoughts as they fly or sail over the Triangle, but how much more intense would be the reactions of a person swimming for two days across the open sea over the Triangle, alone with his thoughts, sensitive to impressions and imaginings, and all the while in direct physical contact with the waters where so many have mysteriously disappeared.

Ben Huggard, of Freeport, New York, is a robust physical-training-oriented police officer (Crime Prevention Unit, Nassau County, New York) not given to imaginative exaggeration or flights of fancy. Nevertheless, Officer Huggard considers that he encountered indications of an alien and inimical force during his swim through the Bermuda Triangle.

Huggard swam within a cage, towed about 150 feet behind a launch equipped with a two-way speaking unit enabling team members to communicate with him or to read with him while he swam. Such reading material included *Jaws*, a book strikingly pertinent to his situation, as hammerhead and other sharks appeared within ten minutes from the start of his swim and continued to follow the cage during the swim. The trapdoor which constituted the entry to the cage was controlled by two double locks, well tested and checked for the swimmer's protection from passing carnivora such as sharks.

Huggard started his epic swim from Sombrero Point, Marathon Cay, Florida, and planned to swim into the current of the Gulf Stream, moving north to help him on his way toward Nassau. He underwent an unusual experience during the night of May 2, 1975, at the end of his first day's swim. At this time the Gulf Stream, or strong eddy thereof, had unexpectedly turned and pulled him southeast toward Cuba, instead of northeast, in accordance with his projected route, taking him many miles off his course. When he was finally able to get out of the eddy or unusual change of current, he began to make good time toward Freeport, Nassau.

As night fell, Huggard, swimming in his cage with the accompanying sharks outside, clearly visible under floodlights from the lead boat, suddenly got the feeling that something was wrong with the trapdoor. In Huggard's words:

I always breathe on the left side. But suddenly I had a strange feeling to look on the right, towards the trap door. As I looked the door opened by itself and fell down, despite the double lock. I swam over and reached up and locked both locks, and tested the door. I then resumed swimming. A short time later I had an urge to look again. While I looked to the right the trap door opened once more. I called for the crew to bring tools to fix the door. They came and tried the locks and said nothing was wrong – nothing could open them. After they went back I kept getting the feeling the door would open again. This went on and on throughout the night with me swimming up and closing the door every 15 minutes or half an hour. I called the crew every time and they must have thought I was crazy because whenever they tried to they could not open it. They shook and pulled it but it never opened. The locks held perfectly. But every time I looked over at it the locks slowly unsnapped and it opened by itself. I am never frightened in the ocean, but I had this horrible fear that caused me to keep looking over on my right. I had this feeling that something wanted me to come out through the door. It was like someone telling me to jump out of a window from a high building. I knew what would happen, with the sharks outside, but the urge was almost irresistible. Finally, when I felt almost forced to swim out, I swam over and grabbed the trap door. I was shaking but I held onto it. I kept saying to myself: 'I'm not going out ... I'm not going to let it take me out of the cage, whatever it is....' and then I slammed it shut.

According to Huggard it did not open again, even during an unscheduled change of weather that temporarily separated Huggard from his cage.

From a tranquil state of clear, calm, windless weather, 'an incredible wind came out of nowhere,' buffeting the cage with eight-foot waves. Request was made to Freeport, Bahamas, for weather conditions ahead and the reply was 'Weather perfect. Clear sailing to Freeport,' although gusts of hundred-mile-per-hour winds where Huggard was swimming suggested to him that, 'Freeport should ask me what the weather was.'

The constantly high winds began to dump Portuguese men-of-war into the cage and, as Huggard had been stung already and feared fatal results from multiple stinging, he swam over a wave which reached the cage, and suddenly found himself outside, landing on top of an accompanying white shark. He got back into the cage before the shark reacted and the swim continued. He eventually reached Cat Cay, Bimini, just as the cage sank, its styrofoam flotation having been damaged by the unexpected and peculiar localized storm.

In response to the inevitable question about whether his misadventures had something to do with the Bermuda Triangle phenomenon, Ben Huggard replies:

I personally believe there is something out there. How can you explain all these things and what has happened to all those people? There has to be a reason for it, but I don't know what it is.

Ben Huggard's experience is especially interesting in view of possible psychic connotations connected with the disappearance of crews from shipboard in the Triangle, during the last 150 years and possibly over an even earlier period.

There are, of course, many possible explanations for the finding of deserted ships and yachts, although the number of them in the area of the Triangle seems to point to an extraordinary incidence of disappearances wherein cargo and even personal possessions were found on board but no sign of passengers or crew. Normal, instead of paranormal or psychic explanations, would include piracy, cargo hijacking, desire of an owner to change identity, conspiracy to defraud insurance companies, kidnapping of the owner and crew (or of the owner *by* the crew), mutiny, waves taking *all* the crew off the decks during a storm, a sudden spreading of fire which threatened a volatile cargo, causing the crew to abandon ship and then lose contact with it, (as has been suggested, for example, in the famous case of the *Mary Celeste*), abandonment of the ship as it appeared to be about to founder in a storm but later inexplicably righted itself (or even regained the surface), to be found later abandoned.

An unusual reason for one famous disappearance, that of the circumnavigator Joshua Slocum in 1909, has been suggested, namely that Slocum, unable or unwilling to get along with his wife, perhaps planned his disappearance in order to escape into another identity at another port. While this was never confirmed, it may not have been the first, or last, planned disappearance for the same or similar reason.

While all of these explanations are possibilities, the numerous disappearances of persons from surface craft, from beaches, and from cars parked near beaches, survivors in the water, and custodians from lighthouses have given rise to a theory that there exists, among the forces within the Triangle, a sporadic influence which affects the human psyche, sometimes impelling it, as, for example, in the case of Ben Huggard, to expose itself to destruction or other unknown dangers.

The theory of inimical influence over the mind was recently the subject of considerable international comment when an Indonesian crew member of the German freighter *Mimi* (Panamanian registry) on October 9, 1975, while the ship was sailing between Miami and Cuba en route to Georgetown, Guyana, suddenly knifed to death the German officers on board, the captain and three others and then opened the sea cocks and sank the ship. Escaping in a lifeboat with other Asian members of the crew, the alleged murderer, Gugun Supardi Suleiman, was later picked up at sea and proved to be tractable and co-operative, although conscious of his actions. When confronted by United States Coast Guard officers he observed, 'We love the Germans. Why should we wish to kill them?' – a somewhat rhetorical question indicating, perhaps, a temporary mental seizure called, in Malay, *amok*. Although it is probable that the cause of his running *amok* was resentment of orders, the fact that a psychological explanation of the influence of the Bermuda Triangle has been subsequently adduced in the case is illustrative of the spreading interest in, and concern about, suspected forces – natural or alien – in the area.

These forces, whatever they are, give evidence of causing unexpected modifications of our accepted laws concerning matter, gravity, space, and time.

CHAPTER SEVEN

THE OTHER SIDE OF TIME

One of the more baffling mysteries of the Bermuda Triangle is the occasional curious loss or gain of time, an especially troubling phenomenon to a culture such as ours, where belief in the measured forward march of time is so unshakably sacrosanct. This phenomenon has been noted principally by aircraft personnel, an understandable preoccupation, since flight time on planes is so carefully recorded, although it may also have a bearing on the mysterious disappearances (and appearances) of ships, old and new, as reported over the years.

Unexplained early arrivals of planes in the area have occurred sometimes after the aircraft had flown through mist or heavy fog. Unexpected early arrivals of planes would be understandable, of course, in the case of extremely strong tail winds – perhaps with wind velocities of several hundred miles per hour – although in most cases there was no strong tail wind present. Another possibility would be the misreading of wind velocity by the pilot, or malfunctioning instruments, although this would not be a common factor in all cases recorded. Some incidents, moreover, have been so carefully cross-checked that it appears that, for a certain period, time was inexplicably advanced, collapsed, or projected into the past – or perhaps future – for the craft and personnel who happened to find themselves in a certain area of the Triangle at a certain time.

Bruce Gernon, Jr, of Boynton Beach, Florida, underwent an unusual experience on December 4, 1970, on a flight from Andros Island to Palm Beach. The incident, although suggestive of space-time warp and 'capture' by a cloud formation is supported by his log, his co-pilot, ground personnel, and even gas receipts. Gernon is a licensed pilot with about six hundred flying hours mostly between the Bahamas and Florida. He is twenty-nine years old, six feet tall, solidly built, with a matter-of-fact approach to flying. His good memory for detail is especially relevant to the unique occurrences of the flight.

Gernon, accompanied by his father as co-pilot, had taken off from Andros flying a Beechcraft Bonanza A36 over the Bahama Banks, en route to Bimini, and while he was climbing to his designated altitude of 10,500 feet, he noticed an elliptical cloud in front of him.

It was sitting there harmlessly, not moving. I was filing my flight plan so I did not think about it or I would have realized that it should have been much higher. I flew over it as I climbed up 1000 feet per minute but I noticed that it rose exactly as fast as I was rising. Sometimes I would get ahead and then it would catch me again. I estimated it as about 15 miles wide. I considered making a 180° [turn] and try to get back to Andros but finally broke through and the sky was clear.

But when I looked back at the cloud I saw it was now gigantic, and was curved in a giant semicircle, with another part of it in front of us, about 60,000 feet high. The bottom of the cloud seemed to go right into the ocean, not like other cumulus clouds that have precipitation or space under them.

Gernon tried to fly around it but found, to his consternation, that he was now inside the 'hole' of a gigantic 'doughnut' cloud, looking for an exit. Finding an opening, he raced for it as it grew smaller, finally diminishing to a cylindrical hole or tunnel in the unusual clouds. By the time he reached the hole, at a critical air speed of 230 miles per hour, it had decreased to about 200 feet in width and was still growing smaller.

It was like looking through a rifle sight. It appeared to be a horizontal tunnel about a mile long and aimed toward Miami. At the opposite end I could see clear blue sky between the tunnel and Florida....

Gernon gunned his plane at critical speed through the tunnel. He noted that the walls of the tunnel were glowing bright white. The narrowing walls were clearly defined and small puffs of cloud were slowly revolving *clockwise* around the walls.

If it were not for the automatic pilot keeping the wings level to the horizon, I would have probably turned the wings with the rotation of the clouds and flown sideways into the walls.

During the last twenty seconds the wing tips touched the walls on either side. At this point Gernon experienced complete zero gravity during a period of several seconds.

When he came out of the tunnel, Gernon found himself to be in a dull greenish haze instead of the blue sky he had previously seen. Although potential visibility seemed to extend for several miles, 'Nothing was visible – everything was the same greenish-white haze.' Attempting to fix his position, he found that all electronic and magnetic navigational instruments were malfunctioning and he was unable to make contact with radar control.

According to Gernon's flight time he should have been approaching the Bimini Keys. Suddenly what seemed to be an island shot by on the haze beneath the plane at a tremendous rate of speed. Then the Miami radar control came in on the radio and reported that a plane was flying due west over Miami. Gernon told the control that he must have identified another plane, as the Bonanza, according to flight time, should be still over the Bimini Keys.

At this point a most unusual event took place.

Suddenly huge slits [in the haze] appeared all around us, like seeing a view through a Venetian blind. They ran parallel to our direction of flight. The slit became larger and larger and we were able to identify Miami Beach directly below us ...*

After Gernon landed at Palm Beach, he noticed that the flight had taken only forty-five minutes instead of the normal seventy-five minutes, even though the flight had been indirect and had covered 250 miles instead of the regular 200 miles. The question remained: How could the aircraft cover 250 miles in forty-five minutes with a maximum cruising speed of 195 miles per hour?

Gernon went deeper into the matter. He checked gas receipts from previous flights and found that the plane customarily used an average of forty gallons for the same trip. But on this trip only twenty-eight gallons of gasoline had been consumed. In Gernon's words: 'This would account for the half hour of time missing, since the *Bonanza* would use 10 gallons of fuel to fly for 30 minutes and would travel about 100 miles.'

Although he has no certain explanation for this time slip, Gernon suggests that while he was in the tunnel the cloud formation may have been moving at a velocity of a thousand miles per hour, which, added to his own speed, would give his plane a speed of 1,180 miles per hour and also account for the saving of gasoline. He also points out the eerie coincidence that Mike Roxby, a pilot from Merritt Island, Florida, was recently killed after his small plane entered a cloud and then crash-landed – as well as the fact that an inordinate number of other lost flights were last heard from in December, in the late afternoon, in the same area. And we remember that Gernon's flight took place on December 4, starting at three o'clock in the afternoon, a chilling reminder of Flight 19, which flew off to oblivion at 2.15 P.M. on December 5, exactly twenty-five years ago less one day.

Reported inexplicable variations in clock time are some-

---

* A several-minute flight from Bimini to Miami would be an impossibility for Gernon's plane.

times shorter than Gernon's lost half hour, and sometimes perhaps vastly longer. A short but striking one has been described in an earlier study; that of the missing ten minutes on a National Airlines flight to Miami. Lost on radar for ten minutes, prior to landing operations, the plane reappeared and made a normal landing. The pilots, already puzzled by the foam trucks, ambulances, fire trucks, etc., on the field, were questioned by the tower and rescue personnel as to whether they had encountered difficulty while they were off radar. According to the pilot and co-pilot nothing had happened, except that they had flown through a haze for about ten minutes. Upon persistent questioning about their radar disappearance the pilots consulted their watches, noticed that they were ten minutes slow, then checked the plane's chronometer, the watches of the non-flying personnel, and made a discreet check among the passengers, and found that all timepieces had inexplicably lost ten minutes, apparently the exact time they had been off radar. Although radar sometimes develops functional peculiarities, the unanimity of the watches suggests the possibility that for a certain suspended period the plane and its passengers *were* somewhere else – in another part of time.

Time bent in another way for the crew of a Navy P-2 in June 1970 returning from a training flight operation involving the tracking of a Russian submarine operating in Bahama waters. Diving close to the surface and then encountering unexpected turbulence on the way up, the P-2 pilot was forced to apply so much climb power that a cylinder blew and the plane continued on one cylinder. Communication was cut off on all bands. A Mayday signal was sent but not acknowledged. Shortly after sending the Mayday the P-2 landed successfully at Jacksonville, where the pilot was asked if he wanted to help look for a plane in distress from which a Mayday call had been received; in other words, to volunteer to look for himself! Somehow, the Mayday call he had sent had been frozen somewhere in the atmosphere (or in time) for a period of fifteen minutes.

There are many instances where an incredible loss or gain of time may be experienced by a plane without any other unusual phenomena being noted at the time. Tim Lockley, ex-Air Force now living in Dallas, Texas, remembers an experience that happened to him in November 1970 while he was crew chief of a C-130, a U.S.A.F. four-engine turbo-prop:

We were on a NATO mission to Mildenhall, England, via the Azores. As it was late November we were flying the south corridor route, that is, from Pope, North Carolina to Lajes in the Azores. What happened was that we gained three and a half hours in flight over the other planes in our group which were all going to the same place at half hour intervals. There was no explanation. C-130s are simply not designed to fly at that rate. There was no electrical disturbance or anything unusual that was noticeable. I did notice one thing however. During the flight I went up to the flight deck to get coffee, and noted that the ground speed indicator was not jibing with the air speed. The air speed was normal but the ground speed indicated that we were going several hundred knots faster than we should have been doing. There was a lot of surprise when we landed. An officer explained that we had probably flown into the jet stream, but this was not possible because we were not nearly high enough for it. Another thing was that strong tail winds of any sort would have been recognized through instrumentation. But there were none.

You hear a lot of rumours about things like this – when planes fly into 'white-outs' – where the sky and water look exactly alike and you don't know where you are or where you are going. You get disoriented about everything, even about time.

(A phenomenon that seems to have often extended to watches and other time-measuring mechanisms as well as to persons.)

Several of the incidents reported in the waters and coastal areas of the Bermuda Triangle seem to reflect past events (and their sounds) or past presences as if time, at certain moments, could project individuals from the present into the past or otherwise bend the continuum of time in a manner blending the past and present – and perhaps the future as well. While some of these reports verge upon the occult or visionary, one must remember that they have been clearly seen and reported by reliable witnesses who in the course of their duties at sea were not searching for strange phenomena but merely observed what seemed to be happening.

John Sander, a steward aboard the *Queen Elizabeth I*, witnessed such an incident during the fall of 1967. According to Sander:

> I was sailing on the Queen Elizabeth I through the area known as the Bermuda Triangle en route to New York from Nassau. The sky was clear and the sea was calm. I was standing with another steward on the after deck at about 6:45 A.M., having a cup of coffee before starting our day's work. Suddenly I saw a small plane, it looked like a Piper Comanche, some 300 yards away and about 200 yards high, flying directly towards us, on the starboard side. I pointed it out to my companion, Sidney Worthington. All of a sudden, at about 75 yards, it just went completely silently into the water, right near the ship. No splash! It just vanished! It seemed to me that the calm sea had just opened up and swallowed it.
>
> The other steward stayed looking at the spot. I informed the officer of the watch. They turned the ship about and put a boat out but there was no oil slick, no wreckage, no nothing. They couldn't believe us.
>
> What I still can't understand is why there was no splash. I know it is almost unbelievable. But as a practising Christian I would swear on the Bible that what I saw was the truth.

A well-documented case of a disappearing plane, observed not by two but hundreds of people, apparently took place in Daytona Beach, Florida, on the evening of February 27, 1935. As reported by Richard Winer (*The Devil's Triangle*, 1974), a veteran observer of unusual incidents in the Triangle, a 'silvery plane with red and green wingtip lights' was seen to suddenly crash into the sea directly in front of the Hotel Daytona Beach at about 10 P.M. The plane was so close that two witnesses, Mr and Mrs Forrest Additon, watching the sea from their balcony, thought 'it was coming right through our window.' Alerted by numerous other witnesses, Coast Guard vessels and other small craft immediately searched the area close to shore, but without success. But as the plane was seen to go into the sea less than a hundred yards from the beach, it is almost inconceivable that no piece of wreckage (or oil slick) was encountered within a well-defined and shallow area of a then calm sea. Hundreds of people gave the same account and identified the same area. However, since subsequent checking of airports in Florida and as far north as Georgia failed to reveal any missing or overdue plane in the area, the incident, in an understandable desire to clarify what could not be explained, was classified finally as a rumor.

As planes have been observed to slip silently into the sea, so have numerous ships, often of another, earlier age, been observed from the decks of other ships, frequently through swirling mists of fog but sometimes in clear weather. These accounts, of course, are the yarn from which legends of the sea are woven, and the phantom ships of the Triangle and the Sargasso Sea, which lies within its eastern section, have been sighted through the centuries, from ghostly Spanish galleons to the ubiquitous *Flying Dutchman*. Sometimes the sightings have been so clear that they have been reported to the Coast Guard, which, although it does not believe in ghost ships, has an interest in abandoned and drifting vessels of any vintage, whether of modern or ancient construction.

Hadley Doty, a former merchant marine navigator with the United Fruit Company and officer of the Royal Canadian Navy, was aboard the *Cyrus Field* on a cable-laying mission in the spring of 1946:

We were about 15 miles off the coast of Florida. It was a

clear night. All of a sudden a lookout yelled, 'Hard over, hard,' which meant the ship was to change course as fast as possible.

The watch saw a square-rigged sailing ship cut across our bow. They couldn't see anyone on her but there was a light in the captain's cabin aft.

The course alteration was noted in the log and reported to the Coast Guard in New York.

The Coast Guard told us there had been several similar incidents that night between Bimini and Florida. We hadn't thought much about it at the time but after the Coast Guard said they were unable to find out anything about the vessel we started to wonder.

She came out of nowhere and she seemed to disappear just as quickly.

Ghost ships, of course, are not exclusively the property of the Bermuda Triangle and have been frequently reported in seas throughout the world. The *Flying Dutchman*, the sailing ship which, according to legend, was condemned to sail the seas forever with a crew of skeletons because the captain had defied God during a rough rounding of the Cape of Good Hope, has allegedly often been seen in the Sargasso Sea, as well as at many other points, although one may assume that the name has often been applied to any phantom ship apparition observed by nervous seamen on watch.

One very famous and apparently not nervous observer of the ghost ship phenomenon was the former King Emperor of Great Britain, George V. The incident occurred while he was still a prince and on duty as a naval cadet on the H.M.S. *Inconstant* in the Pacific in 1881. After the startling occurrence Prince George coolly made a report of the incident as he saw it in the log of the *Inconstant* on July 11, 1881, a type of entry that certainly naval officers of today would hesitate to make official, even if their reputations for veracity and powers of observation were above question. On board the *Inconstant* a dozen other, nonroyal observers testified that they saw the same thing. The entry made in H.M.S. *Inconstant*'s log reads as follows:

At 4 A.M. 'The Flying Dutchman' crossed our bows. She emitted a strange phosophorescent light as of a phantom ship all aglow, in the midst of which light the masts, spars and sails of a brig 200 yards distant stood out in strong relief as she came up on the port bow where also the officer of the watch from the bridge saw her, as did also the quarter-deck midshipman, who was sent forward at once to the forecastle, but on arriving there was no vestige nor any sign whatever of any material ship was to be seen either near or right away to the horizon, the night being clear and the sea calm.

A most unusual type of 'ghost ship' was reportedly encountered by W. H. Prosser about three years ago in the Bermuda Triangle between Eleuthera and Great Abaco in the Bahamas. While all 'ghost ships' can be categorized as 'unusual,' the oddity about this specific one was its tremendous size and the concentrated glare of its lights, causing Prosser to remember it as the 'Flying Dutchman Hilton.'

Prosser, as he tells of his unusual experience in the *National Fisherman* (Vol. 56, No. 5), was piloting an eighty-five-foot research vessel, the *Undersea Hunter*, en route to Florida from St Croix. Although he had previously ascertained on radar that there were no vessels between his craft and Abaco, he was suddenly blinded by a glowing radiance from his starboard beam 'broad sheets of brilliant illumination – as would come through large areas of glass——' It reminded him of 'a huge resort hotel of several levels,' suggesting such nautical comforts as 'lounges, balconies, and a lighted swimming pool——' In order to avoid a collision with the monstrous craft, presumably at sea level, he kept the wheel of the *Undersea Hunter* firm, on what he considered a parallel course with the brilliant apparition. While he was nervously trying to avoid a collision, he suddenly noticed that the unknown craft had vanished from the starboard beam and had become immediately present off the starboard bow. 'It had moved forward 45 degrees in a matter of seconds.' Then the huge 'Flying Dutchman Hilton' instantly vanished, leaving the night black as before.

This unusual and flamboyant manifestation possessed yet another element of mystery. At no time, despite its close proximity, did it show on the *Undersea Hunter*'s radar screen.

While the testimony of the human eye is subject to all sorts of suggested influences of the imagination, as well as subliminal and retained images, it is interesting to note that, according to one recent report, a photograph taken from a ship during a burst of electromagnetic phenomena showed, upon being developed, something the photographer and other observers did *not* see. The occurrence took place in July 1975 during a research and filming expedition on the yacht *New Freedom* on the open sea about seventy-five miles northeast of Bimini. No other ships were in the vicinity. An electromagnetic storm of peculiar intensity was taking place without accompanying rain. The clear evening sky was being constantly illuminated by flashes of lightning, much of it tinged with green and purple. The flashes and the echoing thunder seemed to be building to a crescendo and finally culminated in a blinding lightning pattern on the horizon that seemed to split the sky.

Dr Jim Thorne, director of the expedition, who was taking color pictures at the time with a Pentax 35 mm., had his camera pointed at the horizon at the exact moment of a culminating series of flashes and echoing earsplitting thunder. He was curious to see whether he had captured the phenomenon on film. When it was developed, however, it appeared that he had captured more than he had expected. For what seemed to be the sail of a large square-rigged sailing ship appeared on the left of the print, within seventy-five to a hundred feet of his own ship, the *New Freedom*. But there had been no ships nearby before or *after* the electric storm. The intensity of the flashes on the horizon, of course, would have held the attention of most of the crew, but the camera, devoid of emotion, simply photographed what was in view, however temporarily.

Equipment and developing errors have been ruled out by film experts and developing technicians. There has been no evidence of equipment malfunction or, as yet, any explanation of how a sail and what appears to be part of a wheelhouse of an old sailing ship 'materialized' and were photographed at the exact climax of the intense electric storm.

There may be several reasons why so many 'ghost ship' sightings have been reported in the Triangle through the years. Some may have been suggested by past incidents of violent and adventurous history – others by uncertain shapes discerned at night or through a fog. But while past sightings depended on ocular observation, the phenomena of the present can be checked with precise electronic equipment which has frequently detected before they can be observed or even those which have not or cannot be seen. The *Yamacraw* incident (page 77), where a straight 'land line,' where no land should be, was first detected, then observed, and finally penetrated by a Coast Guard cutter, and which turned out to be a peculiarly straight and high sulfurous fog of sufficient density to affect radar, belongs to this last category. The case of the buoy tender *Hollyhock*, however, whose radar consistently reported land or an island in the open sea miles off the United States coast between Bimini and Florida, may be something quite different. And it should be noted that various civilian yachts have occasionally reported radar land 'sightings' in the same landless area of the Florida Straits. But once land *was* indeed there, at approximately that place in the ocean at a point in earth time relatively not so long ago, when before the melting of the last great glaciation (circa twelve thousand years ago) the coastline of Florida extended far out into what is now the Atlantic Ocean and the Bahama Islands were far greater in extent than they are today.

If, as has been theorized, it were possible, in certain areas among which the Bermuda Triangle may be an especially sensitive example, and impelled by currents or forces that are not presently understood, for time apparently to bend or project visual capsules or memories of the past into the present time, then what may have been somehow perceived in the above cases was perhaps the sight of a ship or other object on its past (or future?) course, or even the visual memory of a lost coastline – or a vanished continent.

Time has apparently stood still for certain radio transmissions; some radio messages and even an occasional television program having been picked up years after they were transmitted, as if they had spent the intervening period floating in time and space.

Such transmissions from the past have been reported by Air Force radio operators on duty in Vietnam who claimed that some of the messages they received were from planes operating in an earlier war – that of Korea. While such reports could come from a variety of causes, including practical jokes, it would be difficult to explain an unusual incident concerning a TV program which occurred in England on September 14, 1963. In this case, British viewers, while watching their TV programs, were surprised to notice that they were fading and were being sporadically supplemented by a broadcast from TV-KLEE, a station telecasting from Houston, Texas. The two telecasts would fade on and off with the Texas one generally coming in more strongly than the British program. The TV-KLEE program in question, however, had been transmitted *several years* previously, and the station itself was no longer in existence. An electronic firm was later employed to investigate the incident but did not arrive at a satisfactory explanation. The name of the company, strikingly appropriate to the mysterious and somewhat lost-in-time aspect of the incident, was the Atlantis Electronics Ltd, of Lancaster, England.

As far as viewing the distant past is concerned, an example can be observed by anyone on a clear night, looking upward at the stars with the realization that the light from many of them, although clearly visible, is no longer really shining. Although the sun that once emitted this light has long ceased to blaze, the light from it, because of the distance the light must travel, is still visible aeons after its source has vanished. Perhaps, taking into consideration the theoretical curvature of light and space, something comparable may happen in the neutral whiteness sporadically occurring in highly magnetized areas of the sea as well as at the earth's poles.

A curious legend has arisen, based on the overflight of the South Pole accomplished by Admiral Richard E. Byrd in 1929. It concerns a radio report allegedly broadcast by Admiral Byrd while in flight – a report so incredible that it was officially silenced – the substance of the report concerning a sighting allegedly made by the Admiral in the vicinity of the pole. During his flight, which was being simultaneously broadcast, he suddenly emerged from a fog and found himself flying over a land free of ice and was able to distinguish vegetation, lakes, and what seemed to be animals resembling mammoths or huge buffaloes and also men in the vicinity of the animals. According to certain interested sources in the fields of zoology and exploration who attempted to follow up this report, the transmission was interrupted and the parts of the radio broadcast containing the unusual references were later excised. Popular credence in this unusual report, however, was later reinforced by Admiral Byrd's peculiarly phrased references to 'that land beyond the Pole ... the center of the great unknown ...' and, even more strangely, a reference in 1957 to 'that enchanted continent in the sky, land of everlasting mystery ...'

The fact that many persons seem to remember, or think they remember, the excised broadcast has provided a mystery within a mystery, including not only the question of what Admiral Byrd saw or was alleged to have seen, but what happened to the original report as well as a reported pamphlet written by Admiral Byrd, comprising less than a hundred pages describing his experience and which has disappeared from libraries and collections although, as in the case of the broadcast, there are still people who claim personal knowledge of this printed pamphlet.

The search for aural witnesses for this controversial and almost legendary broadcast is understandably difficult,

since many people recall it but few are precise in their re-
collections. In this investigation a fortunate development
has been the opportunity to record the testimony of Emily
Ingram, of Miami, a court reporter whose occupation has
trained her memory to considerable precision in recalling
past events. Emily Ingram is a vivacious woman of a lively
nature and a sense of humor, who still functions as an
efficient court reporter after a long career. Her memory of
the Byrd broadcast from the polar flight goes back to 1929.
Emily Ingram recalls the incident in considerable detail:

We were living in Boston then and my father had recently
purchased a new radio which had a loudspeaker as well as
earphones. It plugged into the wall and had a large aerial.
I remember the aerial because my dad fell off the roof
while he was putting it up, but he finally got it working.

My mother was especially interested in listening to this
broadcast from Admiral Byrd. It had been announced that
he was going to follow the 70th parallel over the pole and
that the flight would be broadcast as he did it. We got the
radio station – it was a Boston station – and started listening to the broadcast over the loudspeaker. There was a lot
of static and then we heard Admiral Byrd's voice. At first it
was more or less routine, describing the flight over the snow
and ice. Then the static increased again and suddenly the
static stopped. Everything became quieter and then Byrd's
voice came through quite clearly. Suddenly he was saying:
'Look! Do you see it? There is grass down there ... the
grass is lush ... how green it is ... there are flowers all over
... they are beautiful ... and look at the animals ... they
look like elk ... the grass is growing up to their bellies ...
and look! ... there are people too. They seem surprised to
see a plane.'
I remember at this point that my mother said: 'I'll bet
they have long ears too!' Then there was a lot of noise and
static and that was the last we heard of the program. We
could not get it again and then music came on the same
station without any announcement.

We never heard an explanation about what happened.
Some of our neighbors heard it too but they didn't know

anything either. Admiral Byrd seemed to have been cut off in the middle of what he was saying. I was very interested to learn what had happened so I wrote to the Byrd family in Virginia – you know, the Senator – but I never received a reply from them.

This unusual recall of a broadcast made so long ago emphasizes the incredibility of the broadcast report (as noted in Emily Ingram's mother's initial reaction) and therefore the possibility that the Boston station, on orders from some authority or other, cut off the program as it appeared to be getting out of hand, partially to protect the Admiral's reputation and possibly also because the information was so unusual that censorship, or at least a delaying action, was indicated.

An alternate possibility might be that, if Byrd had flown through magnetic fields, as the interval of concentrated static had indicated, then the cutoff of the broadcast would have been caused not by governmental but by magnetic interference.

On the other hand, if Admiral Byrd had, as some researchers have suggested, penetrated a time warp after passing through areas of intense magnetism, the radio waves would be unable to pass interdimensional barriers which would also give the result of radio malfunction. We have therefore a variety of reasons why Admiral Byrd's broadcast may have been cut off but no acceptable explanation for what he allegedly reported seeing and describing in what should have been the empty white wastes around the pole.

The memory of Admiral Byrd is often associated with this unusual but persistent legend, which has later also included somewhat similar sightings in both the arctic and the antarctic. According to alleged accounts by Byrd to fellow explorers, sightings were made of great beasts, mammoths, and the Pleistocene bison, enormous deer, and human beings. It has been suggested that the Admiral's later odd references to these sightings as well as the 'continent in the sky' were perhaps caused not only by a confused memory of his earlier flight but also as a result of his physical trials during a lengthy and solitary survival test to which he had subjected himself during the long antarctic night in 1934. During his long isolation he had suffered deleterious effects from loneliness and apparent carbon monoxide poisoning, which may later have impaired his observation to the point of suffering hallucinations as he flew over the antarctic wastes at the bottom of the world, where the whiteness, glare, and ofttime lack of horizon are propitious to mirages and other distortions of vision. In this connection it is notable that during the antarctic polar expedition of 1947 a plane flying in complete white-out with malfunctioning panel instruments (one is reminded of the white-outs in the Bermuda Triangle) miscalculated its altitude and crashed with its crew of four.

In subsequent flights over the South Pole in 1947, however, other qualified observers shared Byrd's observations of some surprising polar phenomena. These include the fact that the atmosphere above the pole has only half the density of the rest of the earth's atmosphere and that air, as tested in meteorological balloons, inexplicably grows warmer as it rises in the vicinity of the South Pole. In the words of Admiral Byrd: 'The South Pole is muffled in a warm blanket.'

As there are, in fact, several areas of the Antarctic Continent without ice (one being an iceless level along the Knox Coast with pea-green lakes and brown mounds), it is perhaps possible that an explorer flying over this area might, in his surprise at seeing open land in the antarctic, people it with forms of life other than the usual penguins, although this would be unlikely in the case of such an experienced explorer as Admiral Byrd.

While it is generally accepted that Admiral Byrd noticed something unusual during his flight, over both poles, a legend has since arisen, suggested perhaps by ancient beliefs, that there are great caverns within the earth (or that the earth itself is hollow) and that entrances to these caverns of inner earth may exist at the somewhat flattened parts of the globe at the two poles. (It is to be noted that Admiral Byrd is credited with making a second flight over the North Pole some years after his first one in 1926, and it was during this second flight that he experienced magnetic anomalies and distortion of vision.) According to this point of view Byrd would have flown over a declivity in the vicinity of the pole at a point where he allegedly made his surprising observations. These legends of an inner earth, vividly and picturesquely described in Hindu and Buddhist religious literature and generally believed in Mongolia, Tibet, and contiguous lands of Eastern Central Asia, describes Arghati, this hidden land within the earth, as the home of demigods and men who occasionally ascend to the outer earth. Arghati, this prototype of Shangri-La, has been through the ages a constant object of quest by rulers, travelers, explorers, and mystics in Asia and elsewhere, and even Hitler, appraised of Arghati by some mystics in his service, at one time joined in the hunt and dispatched several teams to search for entrances to this secret hidden inner world.

Notwithstanding the attractive potentialities of this legend as well as the climatic implausibility of caverns or entrances at the poles, it may nevertheless be observed that the visions reputedly seen by Admiral Byrd and others take place in areas of marked magnetic concentration or aberration. Therefore, if Byrd did indeed glimpse men, animals, and vegetation of another age as he flew out of a mist, the locations of such sightings becomes less implausible when we consider that the very land in question was covered with vegetation and animals at another point in time, when the poles were located at places different from their present location, during their many known shiftings over the millennia.

Given a combination of certain natural forces including shifting fields of electromagnetism, it might be possible for a visual observation, hearing, and even electronic equipment to pick up physical memories or replays of incidents such as some of the occurrences described above – voices, sounds, radio and television programs picked up minutes, hours, or years after they were sent, sightings of land in the open sea where there is no land but where land once was, vegetation, animals, and men where now there is nothing but ice, ships long vanished that are still seen to sail, and unidentified and sometimes anachronistic planes that soundlessly fly and as soundlessly crash, or the sounds and sometimes the sights of ancient battles re-enacted before hundreds of witnesses.

Perhaps the suggestion of an occasional repetition or a shift in time would tend to explain the frequent sightings of 'ghost ships,' and planes, as well as some of the other phenomena (which we label 'psychic' for want of a better explanation) noted in the Triangle. It might also suggest what has happened to some of the Triangle's 'victims,' for an opening in time might be, in effect, an entrance into another dimension, possibly without a convenient exit, in which the observer might under certain conditions become a part of the time projection in which he found himself. Considered in this concept, the unexplained disappearance of Carolyn Coscio on June 7, 1964 (see *The Bermuda Triangle*), takes on a new and somewhat startling interpretation.

Carolyn Coscio, accompanied by a passenger, Richard Rosen, was, according to her flight plan, due to refuel at Grand Turk Island on her way from Pompano Beach through the Bahamas to Jamaica. At about the time she should have reached Turk in her Cessna 172, personnel of the small airport could see a Cessna 172 circle the island, could hear the voice of the pilot talking to her passenger, but could not make radio contact from the tower. The pilot observed that a wrong turn must have been taken, that the island was not Turk because, 'there's nothing down there.' Then she was heard to express concern about the gas supply and to decide to fly to another island, followed by the curious question: 'Is there no way out of this?'

Nothing was ever found of Carolyn Coscio or the Cessna 172. It is assumed that the plane over Turk Island was hers even though it was not definitely identified. But the question remains: if the observers on Turk Island could see the plane and hear the conversation, why couldn't Carolyn Coscio hear the tower? Why couldn't she see the field and buildings on Turk? Could the explanation perhaps be that, through a singular inversion of time, she was, in effect, looking at Turk Island – but at a moment in time *before* the airport was built?

Perhaps 'time faults' (if at all possible in the first place) are more common than it would seem; certain reports for centuries from different parts of the world have long described something very similar to such a concept. However, as the scientific theories of yesterday have often metamorphosed into the accepted facts of today, it may be that the multiple riddle of time (and remember that the ancient riddle of the Sphinx of Greek legend was basically a riddle of time) may eventually be better understood. Perhaps other factors that may influence the bending of time will be discovered – the conditions for this bending may exist not only in outer space, as has been predicated by Einstein and others, but even on certain parts of the earth's surface.

In former days unexplained phenomena relating to time faults have usually been attributed to magic or witchcraft and in modern times have been classed with the imaginings of science fiction and to the uncertain field of psychic revelation, both of which have foretold the future with somewhat startling exactness. In the case of science fiction there are the unusual hundred-year-old accounts of Jules Verne wherein the submarine *Nautilus* was given almost exactly similar dimensions as our own atomic submarines and moonshots from earth to the moon were described as being based on the east coast of Florida a hundred years before they actually took place. Atomic bombs and their effects were described even in comic strips several years before their use on this planet. The use of atomic fission in warfare and a startlingly accurate description of their effects are a notable feature in the sacred *Mahabharata*, compiled in India several thousand years ago and referring to events occurring thousands of years before its original compilation.

It is obvious that the universe contains mysteries not only unexplainable by us but also inconceivable to our imaginations. Some of the more basic mysteries are not necessarily located in the distant stars but disturbingly closer. These mysteries concern our own incomplete perception of matter, space, and time as well as their interrelations. Some questions, simple and fundamental as they are, are unanswerable, and any answer to them seems unacceptable to the concepts of which we are presently capable. They include: What is time? When did it begin? When will it end? Where did space begin? Where does it end? How can anything be endless? These short and basic questions are unsettling and even frightening. We unconsciously avoid them. They have become 'forbidden' questions (as far as our day-to-day acceptance of our surroundings is concerned) and are incomprehensible to us. Our advanced knowledge and scientific theory have simply restated these unanswerable questions. But it may be that they are simply outside of our *present* understanding, as the atomic theory was to the magicians and geomancers of the Middle Ages. Perhaps, with the widening of our knowledge and perception, our understanding may someday encompass these questions as our minds increase their potential scope.

However, when we infer that such enlightenment and possible control of time and space will come about when we are able to understand the complex relationships of energy, space, and time, we are perhaps falling into an error in supposing that *we* are the only entities that will make this progress within our own section of the universe. Quite possibly other entities are already in possession of and adapted to such knowledge and therefore possess the capabilities of penetrating at will our own space-time continuum for reasons that, despite the increasing number of theories about extraterrestrial or interdimensional visitors, remain unknown. The ubiquitous UFOs, constantly seen with apparently increasing frequency in all parts of the world, seem to be the vehicles of this projection.

But whatever the explanation of UFOs may be – whether a simple case of mistaken identity or secret technological development – whether they come from outer or inner space, whether they are a reflection or even a probe from the past or perhaps from the future, whether they are a product of people's imagination or even a spiritual and/or actual product made manifest by the union of collective minds of observers, it appears to be fairly evident that UFO activities are somehow associated with the phenomena of the Bermuda Triangle and an examination of their reported activity in that area may indicate a connection that has previously evaded notice – possibly because it was so obvious.

CHAPTER EIGHT

WORLDS OUTSIDE – WORLDS WITHIN

While sightings of UFOs have been reported by millions of observers in various places throughout the world, there seems to have been a surprising concentration of such reports within the area of the Bermuda Triangle. In Puerto Rico, for example, in 1972, they appeared with such frequency that monster traffic jams were caused on country roads when great numbers of people, alerted by TV, press, and radio, took to the highways en masse to observe waves of UFOs and their precision maneuvering in the night sky. This happened repeatedly over certain areas and was clearly observed by thousands of persons who realized that what they were watching were definitely not aircraft as we know them. Entire flights of UFOs appeared and reappeared for three months, almost on schedule, over the hills of Adjuntas, in central Puerto Rico, projecting beams of light from their sides, flying in formation at low altitudes of a thousand feet, making precise ninety-degree turns (impossible for aircraft), holding stationary in the air, and then disappearing into nothingness. (An interesting sidelight on the Adjuntas activity is furnished by information contained in the U.S. Geological Survey's map of Natural Gamma Aeroradioactivity of Puerto Rico, indicating magnetic faults and extreme radioactivity or anomalies notable in the Adjuntas area. Another area of frequent UFO sightings, Arecibo, is the site of the U.S. Government's enormous radio-telescope installation, often called the 'big dish.')

Some motorists experienced a further surprise on their way back from the celestial show. At a point between San

Sebastián and Lares the appearance of an enormous low-flying UFO coincided with the stopping of all automobile motors until the craft, issuing orange and red flares or flames, suddenly ascended vertically and disappeared, at which time the motors started again.

During this same period, at Río Piedras, a suburb of San Juan, another huge UFO appeared over an outdoor birthday party, temporarily blinding the celebrants with a greenish-blue light which seemed to emanate from it as it descended to a low altitude (several hundred feet) over the fiesta. Numerous persons in nearby houses also observed the phenomenon as it cruised in a leisurely fashion between two twenty-story high-rise apartments, and passing cars were stopped as their motors ceased to function. Suddenly, in a cloud of red fog, the strange machine rose vertically and then changed its trajectory as it veered toward a nearby power station and then suddenly disappeared.

On the southern coast of Puerto Rico a gigantic, brightly lit, egg-shaped metallic object appeared at night off Santa Isabel at an altitude of about two thousand feet. It was seen by most of the townspeople and appeared to be throwing or sending off formations of smaller luminous metallic objects which flew off toward the north (in the direction of Adjuntas). Others hovered over the town and one lowered itself vertically like a helicopter over a group of watchers who had come out from a local bar but who scattered (back to the bar or elsewhere) as it approached. (In fairness to unbiased evaluation of UFO sightings it should be pointed out that this object was seen by numerous townspeople who were not in the bar.)

During this wave of UFO appearances members of an advertising agency film unit, taking sunset shots to advertise a product, on top of the Hotel Sheraton in San Juan, found that their background film was being spoiled by the increasing luminosity of a bright shining object that seemed to be hovering over the hotel. As the film crew watched, the strange apparition seemed to grow in size and luminosity until it attained menacing proportions, at which point, to the understandable relief of the crew, it disappeared instantaneously. The advertising film was not a loss, however, as it was sold not to the sponsor but to a company (Creative Films) making a documentary on UFO appearances.

Aguadilla, on the island's west coast, experienced an unusual daytime visitation when a flight of smaller UFOs maneuvered over Ramey Field Air Base and was watched by hundreds of people leaving their work at nearby factories and a local hospital.

These unusual sightings continued in so many different parts of Puerto Rico during August, September, and October of 1972 that it almost seemed that the fleets of space, if such they were, were engaging in a planned demonstration, such as the fleets of the colonial powers, during the days of imperialism, used to perform with a view to 'impressing the natives.'

The 1972 wave of sightings is unusual only in the numbers of people who observed them. Appearances of UFOs are so usual on the Florida coast, in the Bahamas, Haiti, the Dominican Republic, Cuba, and other Caribbean islands, off Bermuda and over the seas between that they are scarcely a news item when reported by only one or several individuals. It is only when thousands of people see the same phenomenon that it becomes newsworthy. Even then, considering the frequency of such sightings, they are soon filed away and forgotten. In Cuba, UFO reports are classified and censured, often considered to be some sort of United States aircraft. During the Bay of Pigs invasion, however, unidentified air and submarine UFOs were seen by both sides; in one instance their startling appearance prevented capture of a CIA operational launch by a Cuban patrol boat.

During the 1972 period of frequent sightings over Puerto Rico, some minor incidents concerning small boats occurred which, although receiving comparatively little attention, may have some bearing on the mystery of the many craft found over the years in the Bermuda Triangle, afloat and seaworthy but without their crews. For while more striking

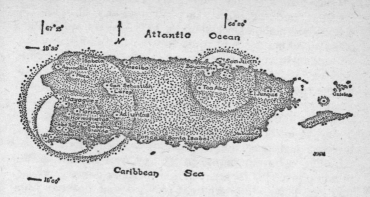

6. *Areas of concentrated and well-documented waves of UFO sightings in Puerto Rico indicate a connection between the frequency of the sightings and magnetic faults or areas of intensified electrification.*

occurrences were being watched in the sky by thousands of observers, several abandoned boats were found in Puerto Rican waters off Mayagüez and floating between Mayagüez and Carbo Rojo. Occupants of these craft were known to have been aboard when the boats left port. About the time of the crews' disappearance, the crew of another craft, a yacht, were startled to observe, in the early evening, a UFO approaching them at a slow rate of speed and at an altitude of less than two hundred feet. As it came closer, before suddenly disappearing, the crew experienced a common sense of terror and several of them attempted to jump overboard before being dissuaded by their comrades. This little-noted incident might possibly furnish one indication of why so many boats are found abandoned within the Bermuda Triangle, in that unreasoning panic might suggest that escaping, even into the unfriendly but familiar sea, would be preferable to staying on board and facing the approaching unknown.

UFO activity along and off the Florida coast is fairly constant, and the objects are often clearly observed. A recent example, on December 15, 1975, was the appearance of an airborne object of some sort which was first tracked on radar without being seen but which suddenly materialized over St Johns River in North Florida and was observed in some detail by the inhabitants of three Florida counties: St Johns, Putnam, and Flagler. Its maneuvers were followed by hundreds of observers including members of the highway patrol and local sheriffs. As it descended and hovered just over the treetops, it was described as resembling 'a burning house in the sky,' as this was the impression given by its great tiers of brightly glowing orange and red lights. It alternately traveled and hovered over places in the three counties long enough for a helicopter to be dispatched from St Augustine. Before the helicopter could get to the area, however, the object was seen to land or approach ground level in Flagler County. Later, after it had disappeared, nothing unusual was noted in the reported area of landing except a high Geiger count. An investigator telephoned Dr J. Allen Hynek, the director of the Center for UFO Studies, in Chicago, to report the incident, and was allegedly told by Dr Hynek to 'be careful of the Men in Black,' a reference to a widespread belief held by many UFO enthusiasts that eyewitnesses of UFO phenomena have frequently been contacted and warned by unidentified persons, usually dressed in black, not to make public what they have seen.

UFO reports received in Florida come from sources ranging from fairly reliable to very reliable (state troopers, pilots, private patrol guards, etc.). These reported incidents range from a whole week of sightings in November 1975 along the Palmetto bypass in Miami and other flights moving over the Miami Palm Bay Club in rows of five at a time (which occasioned an alert to the Coast Guard), to the case of a giant unknown machine tracked by the FAA (Federal Aviation Administration) over West Palm Beach on September 14, 1972. This last incident was also reported by Eastern Airlines observers, police and private individuals, and was further tracked by the FAA in Miami and by Homestead Air Force Base. Planes from the North American Air Defense Command were sent to investigate the shining silver object which disappeared after the airborne planes had got it in view high above them.

Private and commercial planes have reported being buzzed by UFOs in the skies along the coastal routes off Florida and Georgia and at various points in the ocean from Bermuda through the Bahamas and the Caribbean islands. Major Donald Keyhoe, U.S.M.C., Ret., a longtime observer of UFO activity and past director of the National Investigations Committee on Aerial Phenomena, recounts, in *Aliens from Space*, a military report of a near collision between a large UFO and an Air Force C-47 near Tampa as early as August 1, 1946. The object, a long, wingless cylinder with portholes, 'twice the size of a B-29,' came straight toward the C-47 and veered away at the last minute, vanishing at an estimated speed of 1,500–2,000 miles per hour – an incredible speed for an aircraft of that period.

These are but several typical examples (if any UFO activity can be called typical) of some of the more carefully reported or widely observed unidentified airborne phenomena within the bounds of the Bermuda Triangle. It does not suggest the thousands of individual reports of persons in the area who have seen objects or lights in the night sky, of motorists near the shore or persons in surface craft at sea who have experienced a sudden stopping of their motors and cutoff of lights and radio when UFOs passed overhead or, as frequently happens at sea, underwater*; of people walking on or near the shore who, on occasion, have encountered hovering or landing UFOs and been knocked unconscious or semiblinded by a ray suddenly focused on them by the unidentified craft. The increasing familiarity

* The above phenomen was also experienced by the author on May 3, 1975, at about 9 P.M. at a point north of the Tongue of the Ocean, the Bahamas.

of persons in this area with locally appearing UFOs can be illustrated by the reaction of the wife of a radio commentator who, when called outside by her husband to witness an apparent UFO which seemed to be holding stationary at low altitude almost directly over the patio of their house, refused to leave the kitchen, calling from the door, 'I don't want to come to see it. I don't want to know about it. Stay away from it until it goes away.' Although proffered by a housewife, this statement might also be representative of the scientific establishment and governmental agencies when confronted with something, whether UFOs or occurrences within the Bermuda Triangle, which cannot be logically explained.

One wonders whether there is a possible connection between the disappearances in the Bermuda Triangle and the numerous incidents of unidentified flying and submarine objects in the area, noted and reported over the past thirty years. It may be oversimplistic to suppose that if planes and ships are disappearing without trace something on earth or beyond is kidnapping or hijacking them. Major Donald Keyhoe appears to think that UFO aggressive or scouting action has been the cause of the disappearance of certain Air Force planes in this and other areas, but does not specifically link UFO activity with the phenomena observed within the Triangle. John Spencer, a UFO writer and researcher and formally, during service in the Air Force, detailed to U.S.A.F. investigations of UFOs, is 'convinced the UFO explanation is the only logical one' – adding the theory that extraterrestrial beings, desirous of obtaining examples of the technology developed on this planet as well as specimens of the dwellers themselves, have established hidden underwater bases and laboratories on the sea bottom, having chosen this specific Bermuda Triangle area 'because it's the most heavily travelled in the world, both in the air and on the surface' (*Limbo of the Lost – Today*).

The opinion of Dr Manson Valentine, curator honoris of the Museum of Science in Miami and research associate of the Bishop Museum of Honolulu, supposes a certain indifference on the part of extra- or intraterrestrial visitors. Dr Valentine, who has had the advantage, somewhat unique among Bermuda Triangle investigators, of on-the-spot observation of the area for over thirty years, believes that we cannot know and will not know until definite (and perhaps final?) contact is made between us and the operators of the UFOs what their purpose is. He attributes the disappearances of ships and planes within the Bermuda Triangle to fields of ionization set up by the propulsion power systems of the UFOs, which, in his opinion, may be using a form of atomic diffusion instead of atomic fission. This would perhaps explain their incredible speed as well as the probable fate by disassociation or change the molecular structure of craft or individuals who might stray into the ionization fields left by their passage. In other words, they are not spacenapping human beings but are beings simply indifferent to the human entities in their path as they pursue their own particular aims or tasks through our space-time continuum.

Dr J. Allen Hynek, professor of astronomy at Northwestern University, former Air Force consultant on UFOs, and presently director of the Center for UFO Studies, is one of America's leading researchers of UFOs. As far as the question of the Bermuda Triangle is concerned he maintains an understandably cautious attitude about the relationship of the disappearances to UFO intervention: 'I've never been able to find any definite connection between UFOs and the Bermuda Triangle. It would be exciting if there were, but as a scientist I've got to base all my opinions on evidence.'

Whether or not various witnesses' reports of UFO activity at the time of the disappearance of ships and planes would be credited as reliable by Dr Hynek or other investigators, such reports effectively do exist and have existed over the years, like pieces in a jigsaw puzzle which may fit or, again, may belong to still another puzzle.

Albert Bender, former head of the International Flying

Saucer Bureau and the first researcher to publicize the concept of 'the Men in Black,' attributes his first interest in UFOs to reports he heard about huge unidentified aircraft being seen over Fort Lauderdale at the time of the loss of the five Avenger bombers of Flight 19 and the rescue plane that went after them. It will be remembered that the first great popular wave of UFO sightings occurred two years after the incident of Flight 19, in 1947, in the states of Iowa and Washington, where they were called alternately 'flying saucers' or 'piepans.' The UFOs which inspired Bender's curiosity were not referred to as UFOs at the time, a nomenclature that was to be applied to them sometime later. We can only surmise that what one calls them is a matter of indifference to the pilots or occupants of such craft, if they exist, although reports of apparent UFOs seem to have figured in legend and history throughout the ages since the earliest history of mankind. In any case, large unidentified airborne objects, cylindrical or cigar-shaped but definitely not dirigibles, had been reported in the vicinity of Fort Lauderdale in early December 1945, the time of the disappearance of the six planes.

In considering the possibly other-worldly aspects of the incident of Flight 19 one remembers the communications reportedly intercepted by a ham radio operator: that one of the pilots had said, 'Don't come after me – it looks like they're from outer space.' Apparently the first part of this message was picked up on radio communication from Fort Lauderdale, while the second part, if it existed, would have been indistinctly heard because of the intervening static although picked up by the nonmilitary operator on a different receiver. The military interpretation of the 'Don't come after me' message tends to be that the pilot did not consider a rescue operation necessary although the emphasis may have been meant to convey a completely different meaning.

In subsequent accounts of the ensuing search for Flight 19 the loss of the Martin Mariner with its crew of thirteen has frequently been 'explained' by the supposed explosion of the rescue plane itself in mid-air; for various reasons, such as the plane itself being dangerous to fly – 'a flying gas tank,' and that a seaman 'sneaking a smoke' had caused the explosion. Witnesses of such an explosion include the captain and crew of the *Gaines Mills*, who allegedly saw a prolonged explosion or flash in the sky, along the projected flight of the Martin Mariner.

As no wreckage of any kind was noted by the *Gaines Mills* or subsequent search ships or planes and because of a curious hiatus between the time the rescue plane was dispatched and the time it reputedly exploded, it is conceivable that the same flash of light in the night sky, similar to so many subsequent suddenly blazing and quickly fading lights in the same area, could have marked the passage of something airborne quite distinct from the Martin Mariner.

Reports of unusual lights and other phenomena in the area are intriguing, but they remain more of a suggestion than a proof of any connection between UFO sightings and the mystery of the missing ships and planes. While it is true that the years characterized by waves of UFO sightings generally coincide with a high rate of disappearances in the Bermuda Triangle, both the sightings and the losses may be due to a variety of other causes, connected with magnetic shifts, changes in the sea bottom, emissions from the sun or elsewhere, or other unknown cosmic causes. Nevertheless there is still enough coincidence to make the possible connection worthy of consideration.

These 'sightings' during the period and in the vicinity of ship and aircraft diappearances have been variously reported as consisting of traveling lights at night, radar trackings, and occasionally concrete daytime observation of UFOs. When the *Star Tiger*, a British Tudor IV, vanished on January 17, 1949, one of the rescue leads unsuccessfully followed up was that of a reported strange glowing light over the sea in the early morning of January 18. It was never identified. The March disappearance of a U.S. Globemaster coincided within several days with a Navy sighting of a glowing UFO which was also confirmed by radar. Investigation of the case of the Brazilian cruiser *São Paolo*, with its caretaker crew found missing from lines attached to the two tugboats engaged in towing it into drydock on the morning of October 3, 1951, took note of the unexplained lights in the sky glimpsed through a fog during the night of the disappearance. The subsequent intensive air search, while failing to find any trace of the cruiser, made a curious report concerning unusual dark masses of fog or very low-lying clouds concentrated in the approximate area where the ship should have been.

The disappearance of a Navy Super Constellation on October 30, 1954, coincided with several UFO sightings in the Atlantic and coastal air bases as well as, curiously, with a mass UFO 'demonstration' over Rome seen by hundreds of thousands including the then United States Ambassador Clare Boothe Luce. Another series of UFO appearances bracketed the loss without trace of the *Southern Districts*, a tanker, off the South Carolina coast on December 5, 1954 – nineteen years to the day after the incident of Flight 19. The Atlantic sightings were reported by several passenger planes and the objects were described as luminous craft shaped like tops, with portholes, pacing or following the planes and occasionally shining an orange beam on them to the consternation of the passengers and crew. The period of the disappearance of the Antigua-bound schooner *Home Sweet Home* in January 1955 was also marked by a series of reported UFO appearances in the Caribbean and the Atlantic. One of these allegedly shone an orange beam into the cockpit of a National Airlines passenger plane. Several other visitations were reported by Venezuelan passenger planes which were said to have encountered luminous UFOs, also equipped with portholes, in the Caribbean. At about this time a massed flight of an estimated twenty luminous disks appeared over, under, and alongside a Rio de Janeiro-bound Brazilian passenger plane, causing considerable panic among the passengers.

The 1956 disappearances of a B-25 (April 5) and a P-5M (November 8) were also marked by UFO activity in the area of their disappearance. In each case large flying disks were reported in the same vicinity. The crew of an R7V-2 in the vicinity of the B-25 disappearance described a large disk climbing up to the plane's altitude, following or trailing it, and then pulling away. The November 8 appearance, tracked on radar and first thought to be 'a freak weather return,' was later calculated to be an unidentified object '4 to 5 times larger than any known aircraft' and traveling at an estimated speed of four thousand mph.

The incident of the disappearance of the two lighthouse keepers from Great Isaac Light on August 4, 1969, suggests undersea rather than aerial activity: although not noted at the time of the disappearance, a later report from a fisherman, returning from a fishing trip in nearby waters at the time, stated that he had seen fast-moving elongated globes speeding away from the island, clearly visible just under the surface of the sea.

The week after a twin-engine Beechcraft vanished between Jamaica and Nassau on March 23, 1967, a large oval object with a light at each end approached ground level at Crestview, Florida, and was seen to be accompanied by other luminous objects moving through the sky like gigantic pendulums. This was observed by more than two hundred school children and several teachers. The frequent disappearances of planes and ships in 1973 coincided from time to time with the waves of UFO sightings over Puerto Rico and Santo Domingo. Two recent disappearances off the coast of Florida – the *Speed Artist* on December 10, 1975 and the tanker *Imbross* on December 17, 1975 – occurred within two days of the giant UFO seen over St Johns River, Florida.

The answer to the question of whether or not there is a connection between ship and plane disappearances and UFOs must, therefore, be 'perhaps' rather than a definite yes or no. UFOs, whatever they are, have evidently been frequently reported as seen in the same area within roughly the same period of time within which craft have disappeared, although many such craft have disappeared without the reported presence of UFOs which have been sighted throughout the world and over plains, deserts, mountains, and cities as well as over the ocean. Moreover, witnesses have rarely seen ships or planes disappear. What has happened has been that planes and ships have disappeared for unknown reasons after giving their last positions, and it is therefore tempting to imagine, for lack of any other explanation, that something has swooped down on them from space and carried them off. On the few occasions when a ship or plane has been seen to disappear (a paradoxical expression at best), it has first been covered by what appears to be an electromagnetic fog or, in the case of the planes, a cloud into which planes fly but from which they do not exit. This, of course, brings up an alternative possibility, either that the craft fly into unsuspected areas of natural forces which cause them to disintegrate or change dimension or that these areas are artificially controlled cosmic traps for the collection, by unknown entities and for unknown reasons, of specimens of the inhabitants of earth.

According to polls UFOs have been seen by more than 15 per cent of the population of the United States and, evidently convinced by the reports of the 15 per cent, slightly more than 50 per cent of all Americans are of the opinion that these visitors from inner or outer space actually exist. Percentages in areas like the Caribbean, where UFOs are so frequently sighted, are much greater.

Projected on the population of the world at large, whose peoples may be equally or possibly more credulous than the inhabitants of America, we obtain a figure of hundreds of millions who are inclined to believe in the reality of UFOs as evinced by the increasingly frequent sightings reported from all parts of the world. (Jacques Vallée, the French astronomer and NASA scientist, mentions that in China foreigners are often asked if other countries besides China have UFOs.) A conviction that UFOs are not of this world has been shared by many informed individuals of international stature, such as the late Dag Hammarskjöld, who was of the opinion that UFOs were from some other part of the Galaxy, stating that reports from trained observers convinced him that UFOs were probably observation machines from outer space. Belief in the actuality of UFOs was shared by still another Secretary General of the United Nations, the late U Thant, a fitting circumstance, one might say, in that chief officers of a truly world organization were prepared to accept the possibility of encountering and subsequently dealing with representatives of other, perhaps more united worlds.

Prominent public figures in the United States have not hesitated to affirm their belief in or personal sightings of UFOs. In addition to Clare Boothe Luce, who personally observed a large-scale appearance over Rome, Barry Goldwater has seen them in the night skies over Arizona and belongs to the Board of Governors of NICAP (National Investigations Committee of Aerial Phenomena), while Jimmy Carter, who had personally seen one UFO in Thomaston, Georgia, in 1973, resolutely affirmed, as quoted in an interview with the *National Enquirer*, June 1976, 'If I become President I'll make every piece of information this country has about UFO sightings available to the public and the scientists.'

Logical bases for belief in extraterrestrial visitors have been furnished by such specialists as Dr Harlow Shapley, former director of the Harvard University Observatory, when he stated: 'There are at least 100 million inhabited planets. On many of these the inhabitants would be far superior to us,' as well as by the astronomers Drs Otto Struve, Carl Sagan, Frank Drake, and others who, during a project meeting in 1961 at Green Bank, West Virginia, evolved and agreed to a somewhat startling thesis, namely: 'There are between 40 and 50 million worlds which are either trying to signal us or are listening for messages from Earth.'

The French scientist and former NASA specialist Maurice Chatelain has indicated at least three cases of apparent radio signals strongly indicative of the possibility of intelligence-controlled messages from space as if some worlds of the cosmos were trying to make themselves evident to the astronomers of other planets, not through suddenly appearing UFO 'patrols' but through more diplomatically oriented channels.

According to research carried out by V. Troitsky, director of the Gorki Radio Physical Research Institute, and N. Kardashev, chief of laboratory of the Moscow Space Research Institute, repetitive 'code' signals have been received from space over a period of years by four Russian listening stations especially positioned to eliminate local earth signals. They are apparently not coming from our own satellites or probes, as they were discovered years before the first sputnik was launched.

An incident occurred during Project Ozma, the above 1961 operation, carried out in Green Bank, West Virginia, investigating the possibility of the existence of other civilizations in our galaxy. At one point, as the huge parabolic antenna that was being used was turned toward the Whale Constellation, on Tau Ceti in particular, as a possible candidate for civilized development, the receiver, recorder, and the master amplifier were activated, and a series of irregular signals was received. Unlike the regular emissions of the pulsars (which at first were thought to be messages) these coded signals which came on and then stopped were a strong indication that someone or something was sending messages, not, of course, necessarily to earth. The furor caused by this scientific eavesdropping did not last long, however, as security took over and the participating scientists soon decided that they had not heard a message from space.

Starting forty years ago, a series of radio stations in several northern European countries noticed an apparent second echo of their radio signals longer that the customary one seventh of a second and varying up to fifteen seconds as if they had encountered a large object, not the moon, in orbit around the earth. These signals were later followed by the astrologer Duncan Lunan, who, plotting their frequency and the spaces between these apparent echoes, postulated that they could perhaps come from a spacecraft and, if the messages and intervals could be plotted on charts and the code understood, the source of the intelligence sending the messages might be indicated. Following this idea, he stated that he was able to get a plan of a galaxy seen from different angles, namely the Cowherd, and in each graph the star Izar appeared positioned in the middle. (This unusual interpretation of signals, however, assumes that the inhabitants of the planet of Izar would see the universe more or less as we see it – a somewhat doubtful assumption.)

According to the law of averages and probability it does not seem logical to suppose that planetary worlds somewhat like our own have been sending signal probes to the universe at large as we on Earth have also begun to do.

It may be that scientists on other planets are attempting to make contact with other inhabited worlds, or have already done so and what we are hearing are normal intra-galactic messages. By the same token, some civilizations may be so developed that they are able to pass from one solar system to another through forms of projection that we have not yet (other than in science fiction) discovered or even imagined.

This would be an explanation of the apparently extra-terrestrial visits so often noted in the past and present in almost all sections of our planet. But besides an understandable interest on the part of assumed extraterrestrials in intergalactic exploration, the frequency of these visits has raised a certain uneasiness as well as interest on the part of the earth's inhabitants as to their purpose.

Theories are not lacking; a sampling of some of them indicates a considerable variety in observers' opinions, some reassuring and others containing a certain implicit menace.

* They are collecting specimens of local fauna (such as ourselves) and mobile mechanical structures for comparison and study.
* They are from a dry planet and seeking water, which they are taking from the seas of our planet.
* They need other elements, perhaps gold, for their elec-

tronic systems and conductors (there is approximately $360,000,000 worth of gold in every mile of sea water).

* They are protecting us from our innate tendencies to destroy ourselves and our portion of the universe.
* They are keeping air and space travel under surveillance to ascertain that we do not leave the planet on missions of conquest.
* In addition to spacenapping of certain individuals they are studying the behavior of Earth dwellers in their own environment and monitoring communications.
* They are vehicles of undersea humanoids who have developed and lived under the waters of Earth through the millennia contemporaneously and who now, disturbed by the pollution of *their* environment, have decided to take corrective action.
* They come from survivors of a past civilization once established in the Bermuda Triangle and are revisiting their former domain or operating a present one in great domes under the sea.
* They are Venusians who have established a base for future colonization of Earth in the Tongue of the Ocean in caverns below the drop-off near Andros (the pressure on Venus – 91 atmospheres – coincides with the atmospheric pressure at the bottom of the Tongue of the Ocean).
* They are extraterrestrials using the electromagnetic and other natural forces of Earth as an energy supply source for intergalactic and interdimensional travel and regard the inhabitants of Earth and their welfare with cosmic indifference.

All of these presumed reasons for the reported prevalence of UFOs, however, represent invasion syndrome (or, at best, a benign colonialism) on the part of the proponents of most of these theories. In other words, since our own history has been one of constant invasion and conquest, it is only natural to assume that unidentified and technologically advanced visitors have the same thought in mind.

While on the subject of cosmic colonialism, benign or otherwise, one remembers that it has been suggested by Erich von Däniken (*Chariots of the Gods?*) and others that visitors from other planets, possibly Venus, taught the arts of civilization to our primitive ancestors in the early morning of the Earth and that this memory has been kept alive through legends, in Judeo-Christian religious tradition, of direct intervention in the affairs of the Earth from God and the angels (viz., Genesis and apparent references to space-traveling Ezekiel) or, in other cultures, from the gods.

The testimony of ancient cosmic visits is also based on the anachronism represented by the finding of scientifically advanced artifacts dated in so early a period in Earth's history that they appear to be unexplainable; gold ornaments from ancient Colombia that seem to be models for jet fighter aircraft; a geared star computer found on the bottom of the Aegean Sea; a carved tomb covering from Palenque, Mexico, apparently depicting a stylized space capsule; electric batteries in the ruins of Babylon; maps of extreme antiquity showing the exact position of continents that were not to be discovered until thousands of years later, to name but a few, as well as the presence of colossal engineering works of unknown antiquity including four-million-pound quarried blocks in Lebanon; the enormous 'welded' stones in the pre-Incan ruins on the Andean Plateau in South America, and the method of construction and exact astronomical information contained in the Great Pyramid of Egypt.

While this theory of guidance from other planets – a sort of implied 'Peace Corps' – is indeed an intriguing one, it must be evaluated in view of the now apparent extreme age of humanity (it has recently been pushed back from 3,500,000 to 4,000,000 before present) and the various advances and regressions of early and as yet unknown civilizations upon Earth.

If our own civilization, if we calculate its beginning from Egypt and the Middle East, has progressed from primitive herding to the splitting of the atom in only six thousand years, it would seem not unlikely that our own unknown ancestors would have had ample time, between climatic shifts and other catastrophes, to construct not solely one but many advanced cultures without guidance – although probably not without interested observation – from elsewhere in the universe. One theoretical basis for the 'interested observers from outer space' explanation is that such watchers are observing our stages of civilization to determine when we may reach a high enough plane to be worthy of acceptance by and contact with more developed civilizations in the Galaxy.

A rather dramatic note of what may have been a casualty of a cosmic visit or observation about half a century ago has been injected into the UFO controversy by the recent publication of *The Fire Came By*, John Baxter and Thomas Atkins – Doubleday, 1976, wherein what was formerly considered to be a meteorite that had struck the Tunguska region of Siberia in 1907 has been re-examined as a possible atomic explosion of a 'manned' (in the most general sense of the word) space vehicle from parts unknown.

Russian scientists had previously studied the great explosion which was seen as far away as England and the seismic shock registered as far away as Washington, D.C., but had generally supposed it to be a meteorite until recent radioactivity tests and study of the directional force of the blast as well as the size of the area indicated that the explosion came from a point above the earth and that, according to some scientists, it had an approximate energy yield of thirty megatons, 1,500 times that of the atom bomb dropped on Hiroshima.

Retracking its course as far as possible from accounts of witnesses who saw the object tearing through the skies, at various points horizontal to the Earth and to execute apparently a course change, has suggested to investigators that the object was controlled but was also malfunctioning.

The flash and concussion are recalled by witnesses, the mushroom cloud and the black rain after the blast, radiation scabs on reindeer that had survived the explosion, as well as the radioactivity still present in the area, have convinced Aleksander Kazentsev, Soviet author, scientist, and space authority, that the phenomenon was caused by the explosion of an earth-circling vehicle from space, possibly on its way to Lake Baikal in Siberia in search of fresh water from Earth's deepest lake.

While the only casualties of this explosion were the forest and the reindeer in the vicinity, the same blast, occurring over the populated centers of Russia (or of the world) would have wiped out the entire population of any city it burst over, as well as the surrounding areas. The possibility of atomic blasts from outer space, even if by mistake, may represent one more cause for concern on the part of Earth's inhabitants, already preoccupied with their own present threats of atomic warfare or malfunction of atomic-powered equipment.

Major Donald E. Keyhoe, veteran observer and writer on UFOs, (see page 167), is representative of a military viewpoint unofficially shared by many pilots as well as Russian observers who now report UFO activity in the Soviet Union. (It is interesting to note that the Russians, who long suspected Americans as being behind the UFOs, and the Americans, who long suspected the Russians, are now semi-officially reporting to each other.) Major Keyhoe considers UFOs a potential threat coming from space with a special interest in our technology. He thinks that they represent a danger for another rather unsettling reason: the possibility that the Russians or ourselves mistake a flight of UFOs over national territory as a potential enemy and take retaliatory measures with catastrophic results. He astutely suggests that any extraterrestrial sophisticated enough to reach Earth would probably be capable of interpreting television and radio programs with perhaps ominous results for Earth if they decided from our news or entertainment that we were hopelessly committed to violence and should be liquidated before contact. Major Keyhoe therefore suggests that contact should be attempted with UFOs to assure them of our peaceable intentions and that the censorship which he considers has been imposed by government agencies, especially the Air Force and the CIA, be lifted and that the Government should co-operate with civilian forces to attempt to establish peaceful contact with our unearthly visitors.

It is natural that UFOs be considered by observers from individual, regional, or national points of view. Just as researchers of military background, American and Russian, tend to consider the UFO visitation from an 'invasion,' 'attack,' or 'truce' point of view, one is not surprised, considering the religious impetus on the Spanish-speaking world, that the leading Spanish writer and commentator on UFOs (in Spanish they are called OVNIs*) connects them with religious or Satanic manifestations. Salvador Freixedo, a Jesuit priest and prolific writer on the subject, and especially an authority on UFO phenomena in the southwest part of the Bermuda Triangle, suggests that the appearances of and visitation by the devil or devils throughout human

---

* Because of the presence of UFOs in skies all over the earth, it is interesting to note what they are called in the languages spoken over the greatest areas. The Romance languages refer to them as OVNIs, which, literally translated, would be 'objects-flying-not-identified':

    Spanish: *objetos volantes no identificados*
    French: *objets volants non identifiés*
    Italian: *ojetti volanti non identificati*
    Portuguese: *objetos volantes não identificados*

Germans call them UFOs, as is spelled by the initial letters of: *unidentifierte fliegende Objecte*. In Russian unidentified flying objects, although they are only recently beginning to be mentioned, are expressed as *nyepoznanniye l'yekayooch'shiye obyectiy*. In other languages the term is usually a variant of 'flying saucer':

    Chinese: *fei tieh* (fly-saucer)
    Japanese: *sora tobu emban* (sky-fly-disk)
    Malay-Indonesian: *piring terbang* (saucer fly)
    Arabic: *sohhoun taa'ira* (saucers flying)

In the islands of the Pacific such as Hawaii, Tahiti, and others, UFOs are considered by the indigenous populations to be simply a continuation of the lights and objects seen in the night sky over the Pacific for untold aeons: *akuatele* (flying spirits) – a perhaps not inappropriate designation.

history have really been an account of the same phenomenon: what the Church and our ancestors called devils
we call the pilots and occupants of UFOs. Father Freixedo
compares the sulfuric smell, frequently noticed by startled
observers of UFOs, with the well-publicized odor of brim-
stone normally connected with Satan.

He points out that, in the many reports of contact between people and UFO intelligences in the Caribbean, the
UFO entities have spoken Spanish (as they have spoken
English, Russian, French, Italian, German, etc., in other
parts of the world) and have shown a curious tendency to
indulge in 'sarcasm, tricks, [and] pranks, apparently without any special reason and solely for the purpose of annoy-
ance,' a salient characteristic of devils and witches as reported through the ages. Some of Father Freixedo's theories,
especially those that connect past miracles of the Church
and the saints with UFO activity (for 'angels,' according to
Father Freixedo, one may substitute 'good UFOs') have
been contemplated by the hierarchy of the Church with a
pronounced lack of enthusiasm, definitely not encouraging
to his future progress within the Church. Nevertheless, he
has continued to point out that, whenever UFOs are noted
in the Caribbean area, waves of local miracles such as weep-
ing or bleeding church statues, luminous pictures, flashing
rays of light from church towers, remarkable cures of individuals, and other manifestations occur *at the same time*.

Father Freixedo is of the opinion that UFOs do not come
from a point in outer space, but considers them as coming
from points much closer to our own planet or dimension:
'Man is beginning to realize that he is not alone [as an intelligent being] on this planet. It is as if he were living in
one apartment of a condominium – every so often he sees
(or hears) someone from another floor.' Noting that nobody
knows what UFOs want and that 'from our point of view
they seem to be operating illogically,' he feels that UFOs
have caused the deaths of thousands of people in the Caribbean and elsewhere, either by chance or design. ('They are
a force – like electricity. Can one say that electricity is good

or bad?') According to Father Freixedo the UFOs within
the areas, like Puerto Rico, with which he is most familiar,
seem to originate from areas of known magnetic faults and
are seen to follow power lines and to hover over power
stations, using them, if they are interdimensional, as Father
Freixedo thinks, to penetrate our world. In his opinion we
are now coming to a point where contact will be made with
the 'other dwellers in the condominium,' a contact that will
be clearly evident, not sporadic as heretofore, and perhaps
distressing. 'Humanity is approaching a curve in the road
of history, and when a curve is reached in the road the tires
screech.'

Dr Manson Valentine is also of the opinion that some
of the UFOs observed in the Triangle area appear to be
interdimensional rather than from outer space and that
the loud explosions frequently heard during the moment of
their appearance may be one of the side effects of their interdimensional crossings. (Father Freixedo has referred to it
as 'noise from the other floors in the building.') Dr Valentine directs attention to the many reports that, while UFOs
frequently appear unannounced, there is an intermediary
period before their sudden materialization during which
they may be tracked on radar. In other words, they are
there but, possibly because of limits to our visual spectrum,
among other reasons, we are unable to see them. In like
manner, after remaining within sight or on radar screens for
varying periods, they become instantly invisible to the
human eye and instantaneously disappear from the screen.
Dr Valentine, pointing out that 'there is evidence that strong
magnetic fields are capable of generating conditions favor-
able to dimensional release,' suggests that UFOs make use
of such fields and also intensify them. He observes that the
glowing clouds reported at the time of certain disappearances within the Bermuda Triangle may be the result of
the 'materialization' of a large UFO that has generated a
magnetic field of such force that the side effects are perhaps
the cause of many of the recorded disappearances.

Dr Valentine is in agreement with Father Freixedo and

others about the possibility of magnetic faults being a
source of materialization, or point or 'window' of entry of
UFOs, with special consideration given to the seismic and
magnetic faults in Puerto Rico, the Puerto Rico Trench,
directly north of the island, the Tongue of the Ocean (the
hole or pit in the ocean bottom which falls off directly
from the shallow Bahama Banks to a precipitous depth of
more than a mile, between Andros and the Exuma Chain
in the Bahamas), the so-called 'bottomless hole' in the ocean
off St Augustine (an oceanic sinkhole of presently undetermined depth), and another section of the open sea east of
the Bahamas where the surface level of the ocean seems
to go 'downhill' to a depression of 250 feet before rising
again. In the light of investigations scheduled to take place
in the near future, other areas of magnetic and gravitational
faults may be located.

If the supposition of disappearances of persons through
the intervention of unknown entities in the vicinity of
special magnetic fields or seismic faults or a combination of
the two is worthy of consideration, the disappearance of an
entire regiment of British troops in World War I is of
special interest. This incident can be compared, in the
number of people who vanished, with the large personnel
losses of the *Cyclops*, the *Atlanta*, the *Marine Sulphur
Queen*, and other famous disappearances which took place
in the Triangle and, in addition, it is well attested to that
numerous individuals witnessed the disappearance. Although it happened far from the Bermuda Triangle, during
the ill-fated Gallipoli campaign in Turkey, on August 28,
1915, the mention of an encompassing cloud or fog strikes
a reminiscent chord as well as the fact that it took place
along the same lines of latitude and in the vicinity of a
seismic fracture zone. Notwithstanding the confusion and
uncertainty involved with reporting an incident occurring
under combat conditions, the witnesses' report of the unexplained disappearance of the First Fourth Norfolk in the
vicinity of Hill 60, Sulva Bay, is precise, clear – and completely baffling.

Although the entire regiment was listed as missing, witnesses from the ANZAC (Australian and New Zealand Army Corps) and also the Turkish forces claimed that the advancing British regiment never made contact with the Turks. According to observers from the New Zealand No. 3 Section of Number One Field Company, New Zealand Expeditionary Forces, the British Regiment, the First Fourth Norfolk, walked into an unusual ground cloud near Hill 60, Sulva Bay, and never reappeared. Witnesses to the incident noted that the weather, on the morning of August 28, 1915, was excellent. A signed joint statement by Sappers F. Reichart (4/165), R. Newnes (13/416), and J. L. Newman (number not given) describes what they saw:

... The day broke clear, without a cloud in sight ... except for six or eight 'loaf of bread' shaped clouds – all shaped exactly alike – which were hovering over Hill 60. In spite of a four or five mile an hour breeze from the south these clouds did not alter their position in any shape or form, nor did they drift away under the influence of the breeze. They were hovering at an elevation of about 60 degrees as seen from our observation point 500 feet up. Also stationary and resting on the ground right underneath this group of clouds was a similar cloud in shape, measuring about 800 feet in length, 200 feet in height, and 200 feet in width. This cloud was absolutely dense, almost solid looking in structure, and positioned about 14 to 18 chains from the fighting in British-held territory. All this was observed by twenty-two men of No. 3 Section of No. 1 Field Company, NZE, from our trenches on Rhododendron Spur, approximately 2500 yards south west of the cloud on the ground. Our vantage point was overlooking Hill 60 by about 300 feet. As it turned out later, this singular cloud was straddling a dry creek bed or sunken road (Kaiajik Dere) and we had a perfect view of the cloud's sides and ends as it rested on the ground. Its colour was a light grey, as was the colour of the other clouds.

A British Regiment, the First Fourth Norfolk, of several hundred men, was then noticed marching up this sunken road or creek towards Hill 60. It appeared as though they were going to reinforce the troops at Hill 60. However, when they arrived at this cloud, they marched straight into it, with no hesitation, but no one ever came out to deploy and fight at Hill 60. About an hour later, when the last of the file had disappeared into it, this cloud very unobtrusively lifted off the ground and, like any cloud or fog would, rose slowly until it joined the other similar clouds which were mentioned at the beginning of this account. All this time the group of clouds had been hovering in the same place, but as soon as the singular 'ground' cloud had risen to their level, they all moved away northwards, i.e. towards Thrace (Bulgaria). In a matter of about three-quarters of an hour they had all disappeared from view.

The Regiment mentioned is posted as 'missing' or 'wiped out' and on Turkey surrendering in 1918, the first thing Britain demanded of Turkey was the return of this regiment. Turkey replied that she had neither captured this Regiment, nor made contact with it, and did not know that it existed. A British Regiment in 1914–18 consisted of any number between 800 and 4000 men. We who observed this incident vouch for the fact that Turkey never captured that Regiment, nor made contact with it. . . .

While the disappearance of numbers of troops in battle conditions may often be explained by a simple desire for survival, it is no less remarkable that none of these soldiers ever reappeared. If it is possible that the troops of the First Fourth Norfolk Regiment marched off into another dimension, it is to be hoped that their new continuum was to be less menacing than the one they had just left which, as the casualties in the Gallipoli campaign indicated, left but slight alternative to disaster and death. Perhaps the unknown alternative was not altogether unwelcome.

It is fairly obvious that, in the event that collection of personnel or equipment is involved, both could be more easily sequestered without notice in times of war than in times of peace. Planes and several flights of planes that disappeared over the Bermuda Triangle during World War II did not, understandably, receive the amount of public attention reserved for later peacetime disappearances.

An increase of UFO activity seems to have occurred during the course of recent wars, especially those where aircraft have played an important part. Both sides in World War II thought that the flying lights that accompanied bomber flights (the 'foo fighters') were a development of the opposing air force; this happened in the European theater as well as in the Pacific, and later in Korea and Vietnam. When one considers the above as well as the reported UFO 'interest' in air space shots, one might be inclined to find a certain logic in the theory that supposes particular UFO preoccupation as our progress in potential military destruction continues. Although only two of the some nine hundred atomic explosions have occurred during hostilities, the practice explosions in the skies, seas, and under the Earth may have long echoes and, if other intelligences are watching us, this intense atomic activity on our part might understandably constitute a cause for concern. One remembers that the long series of UFO sightings began shortly after the first atom bombs were exploded, and has continued ever since.

CHAPTER NINE

THE GAP IS NARROWING

In the over-all picture of UFO appearances over the seas, coasts, and lands of Earth there is a basis for the conclusion that incidents are not only occurring with greater frequency but are being witnessed by an increasing number of qualified observers. Meanwhile informed opinion as to the provenance and purposes of the UFOs has undergone a subtle change.

This change, which might have been first suggested by the distinguished psychiatrist Carl Jung, assumes that UFOs, while real, are also partially a psychic phenomenon. This theory suggests that UFOs, rather than being craft from outer space, are either from this planet or from a contiguous dimension and in some way connected with the psychic potentialities of the viewers. In other words, UFOs depend for their form and visibility on the collective consciousness of those who see them, which may vary with individuals. Well-known researchers, such as John Keel, a longtime investigator and writer on the subject; Jacques Vallée, the French astronomer and physicist; and Dr J. Allen Hynek, who might be referred to as the present 'dean' of UFO investigation, no longer are convinced by the simplistic explanation that UFOs are raiding space ships from the Galaxy or beyond. According to these new theories, they may be coming from a point much closer to us – or they may be already here, in a contiguous dimension, although visible only when they come within our spectrum of color visibility, range of sound perception, or time sphere. Vallée, drawing on his own background of, and access to, French and Celtic legends, suggests that fairies, elves, gnomes, and other magical apparitions are not necessarily 'fairy tales' but incidents which have occurred through the ages. Witnesses ineptly described what they thought they perceived, which would now be referred to as UFO visitations. In the same way as Father Freixedo has explained the numerous activities of the devil through the long annals of religion, Vallée points out that fairies, pixies, and their like are equally infamous for the annoying tricks they are reputed to play on people as well as their habit of deception and of not being what they appear to be, just as the UFO entities are now being reported to indulge in apparently aimless, annoying, confusing and illogical behavior as they make themselves increasingly apparent to the peoples of Earth.

John Keel, commenting on reported actions of UFOs, has proposed an unsettling theory: the sentient entities of the UFOs or their possibly computerized intelligence are something beyond our five senses and therefore cannot be judged according to our normal context of sanity. If UFOs are operated by intelligent entities, one wonders why they seem to behave so erratically; appearing out of nowhere, disappearing instantaneously, allegedly making contacts with individuals or small segments of the population, apparently at random, sometimes abducting and sometimes releasing people in various locations among which the Bermuda Triangle may perhaps be one of several convenient collection points.

Dr Hynek proposes an ingenious and rather logical explanation as to why UFOs appear to be so reticent in making direct contact with governmental or military authorities in the area of operation. (It should be pointed out that several alleged 'shoot-outs' between UFOs and American and Russian planes – all fatal to Earth's representatives, and a UFO and an American surface vessel in the South Atlantic – we won – are certainly one form of direct contact although not a manifestly diplomatic one.) In Dr Hynek's hypothesis, UFOs have been approaching us çautiously over a lengthy period. Suppose, reasons Dr Hynek, that we ourselves found other civilizations on other planets – if we made ourselves manifest immediately, the inhabitants might receive a cultural shock from which they might not recover – they would react with 'utter panic or abject worship'; while if we took time to enable the cosmic natives to become generally aware of our presence, advancing and retreating over many years and, meantime, studied their habits within their own cultural continuum, the eventual dislocation, after the superior culture finally made definite contact, would be less traumatic.

Ingenious as the explanation appears to be, the considerate approach to avoiding a cultural shock to the 'discovered' inhabitants has certainly not been a typical attribute of past explorers of the Earth as the near extermination of the original inhabitants of the Americas, Australia, and the South Seas may witness. It is to be hoped that the planetary explorers may be more altruistic than our own explorers. But there is no certainty of this, however comforting though the thought may be that minds capable of great scientific advance must be above primitive ideas of conquest and destruction.

A salient factor about UFOs is that concrete knowledge about them is totally lacking. Until other than hearsay haphazard contact is made with them, we cannot know why they are here or what are their projected relations or plans with the present inhabitants of Earth. It is also impossible to tell whether they are connected with each other or whether they come from different sources; some from the Galaxy, some from inner space – worlds within worlds – or from an even more unusual source, almost unacceptable to our frame of reference.

This last possibility, suggested in part by the persistent, ephemeral, and seemingly aimless appearances of UFOs, is that they come not from space, caverns in the Earth, nor from under the sea, but from another era of time – they might be piloted by our own descendants or by our remote ancestors, whose civilizations, different but not necessarily inferior to ours, may have flourished in great centers now covered by the ocean.

In the latter case, coming as they might from outside of time, they would be beyond our vision no matter how powerful our telescopes. On the other hand, if they were crossing over through a dimensional pathway from another world, coexistent with ours, they would also be beyond our range of colors, sound, or perception of matter, at least until they suddenly appeared within our own visual spectrum.

A pertinent question often posed by anyone puzzled by the persistent and constantly more detailed reports of UFOs concerns their purpose and their intentions toward the present dominant species of our planet – ourselves. If those within or behind the UFOs have superior powers, one wonders why they do not appear and land at one of our great centers, assume a 'take us to your leader' attitude, and make their intentions known. For hundreds, even thousands of years a series of flying objects have been seen in the sky, immortalized in legends, later recorded in contemporary writings, and finally, in our day, become a familiar feature in thousands of police records, press articles, and reports from planes and ships throughout the world.

While there have been many instances of reported contacts between UFO crews and inhabitants of the earth, and frequent temporary spacenapping of the latter, in no known instance have the crews of UFOs made open, evident contact with a local authority or even with any leading UFO researcher, most of whom would warmly welcome such a gesture. On the contrary their numerous contacts and 'interviews' have allegedly been made with lonely drivers of cars or trucks, ranchers, shepherds, or people walking at night in deserted areas. According to many of the persons who have claimed to have been captured, interviewed, and later released by UFOs, their purposes are specific and, in the majority of cases, the aliens have expressed (through the use of the local language or thought transference) the intention of making open contact in the near future, bringing cures for diseases and panaceas for our other ills.

An intriguing footnote to the above aspects of UFO visitations comes from a report of an incident in Argentina, not far from one of the twelve areas, in this case the 'South Atlantic Triangle' off the coast of southern Brazil, Uruguay, and northern Argentina, predicted by Ivan Sanderson (author and founder of the Society for the Investigation of the Unexplained) as an area of possible point of contact with other worlds. In this case, a seventy-three-year-old Argentinian farmer named Ventura Maceiras experienced a confrontation with a UFO with unusual results. According to Maceiras, at ten-thirty on the evening of December 30, 1972, while he was sitting in his cabin listening to his transistor radio, it suddenly went dead. Hearing a humming overhead, he left his cabin and saw a UFO, seventy-five to eighty-five feet in diameter, a glowing red-orange in color, hovering over a grove of eucalyptus trees at an altitude so low (about thirty-five feet) that he could distinguish its humanoid occupants through large portholes or windows and even the 'inside' machinery of the object. Then the UFO flashed a ray on him, changed color, and disappeared, leaving behind a strong smell of sulfur. As in the case of many other sightings, the trees were blasted in the area of the visit. What was more unusual was the effect on the spectator.

According to Maceiras, he felt a tingling throughout his body as he watched the UFO; afterward he was affected with vertigo and severe headaches. Within several days a great deal of his hair fell out; he broke out in a series of skin rashes and experienced difficulty in talking. As the effects of his experience wore off, he found to his astonishment, and later to the astonishment of the doctors to whom he was taken, that his physical condition had undergone additional changes, this time for the better. He was now growing new hair, this time black instead of gray, as well as a number of new teeth. His appearance was more youthful and his reactions were faster than before. His slowness in conversation left him and, although he was still illiterate, he began with unaccustomed fluency to discuss with his interviewers matters concerning sociology, philosophy, and his concept of the cosmos.

This reported incident of rejuvenation and 'instant education' is rare in UFO encounters, although Ralph Blum, an author who has made a study of American contactees, is of the opinion that a psychic bond exists among them and that their spiritual outlook usually is improved.

Others of the reputed many cures as results of a UFO experience have been increasingly attributed by some writers to the same forces that trigger miraculous cures within an individual when he is psychologically prepared for a miracle, taking into consideration that miracles of curation have occurred in different localities and centers of the world, and certainly not always those of one special religion.

Some observers, such as Keel, Freixedo, Vallée and others are of the opinion that the UFO beings or personalities have been the cause of many famous miracles over thousands of years and that humanity has seen the actual or representational appearance of devils, gods, goddesses, ghosts, and witches because the alien personalities desired that we see what we expected to see, instead of seeing our spatial or dimensional visitors the way they really are. By the same token, in today's preoccupation with space flight, our imaginations are directed to seeing the occupants of UFOs as astronauts, while, at the same time in other parts of the world, other roles are being assumed by space visitors, almost as if it were a game in which we, of course, are not the players but the pawns.

An incident typical of such UFO trickery or 'playfulness' allegedly happened to Carlos Díaz on January 5, 1975, in Bahía Blanca, Argentina. Díaz, a railroad worker, was walking to his home from a bus stop after buying an early morning newspaper at 3:50 A.M., when a strong light flashed on him from the sky and he found himself being physically lifted upward. He lost consciousness during his upward 'fall' and when he regained it he found himself inside a sphere which appeared to be moving rapidly through the sky. During his unusual trip several 'faceless' humanoids seized him and attempted to cut his hair. Díaz, while he struggled, fainted again and woke up in a field outside Buenos Aires about three hundred kilometers away from his bus stop. Hitching a ride to a hospital, he tried to recount his experience, which received some limited credence only when he displayed the morning newspaper from Bahía Blanca, which was not due for some hours in Buenos Aires. Examination in the hospital, where he was considered a security case for several days and visited by dozens of doctors, revealed no damage from his experience except the loss of tufts of hair from his head and chest. Like Maceiras he now claims he can think more clearly and better although, being still young, no recession from old age has been noted or expected.

Díaz's extraterrestrial capture (or vision) is but one of numerous cases throughout the world. Many, especially while they are being studied, are kept under censorship for military or other reasons. Sometimes men and animals are reputedly taken and later released. On one occasion a car and its driver were lifted, transported, and left several hundred kilometers away from Mexico City, where the initial capture took place. This incident implies an unusual choice of specimens for beings whose automotive capabilities must be far in advance of ours.

Since we do not know whether these apparent extraterrestrials really exist or whether we are seeing visions or projections, we are even less able to know what they are looking for or why they are here. A recent puzzling incident was witnessed by a number of people on the night of January 15, 1975, in front of the Stonehenge Apartments, overlooking Hudson City Park across the river from New York City. A spherical UFO was seen to land in the park by observers in front of the building as well as by startled tenants inside the apartments. A hatch opened and, according to the report, small humanoid figures climbed down a ladder. They seemed to dig in the ground of the park with shovel-like objects, fill some containers, get back in the sphere, ascend with a flash of light or flame, and disappear, very much like our astronauts' takeoff from the moon after gathering space rocks. This case has been cited by some UFO observers as another indication of 'camouflage,' first, because we rationally expect to see extraterrestrials take samples from Earth as our own astronauts have done on the moon and, secondly, extraterrestrial travelers would necessarily be so advanced that they would not still be using shovels (although one might argue that, despite all our own progress, a shovel is still an eminently efficient way to get soil samples into a pail).

As if the above manifestation were not enough for the dwellers in the Stonehenge Apartments, three further visits were reported by startled tenants and passers-by during the months of January and February of the following year, 1976, almost as if the extraterrestrials were searching for something (or someone) at a particular place.

Reports still continue to come from different points in the world about activities that UFOs and their occupants are performing on or over our planet. In Florida they have been seen taking up fresh water from inland lakes and springs, again a logical assumption from our point of view. UFOs have also been blamed for the great power blackout on the Atlantic Coast of the United States in 1965, during which, in the absence of all electric light, luminous UFOs were seen over coastal cities in Massachusetts, Rhode Island, New York, and New Jersey, as well as in Syracuse, where an enormous luminous red ball seen by, among others, the Deputy Commissioner of the Federal Aviation Agency. Again, to an observer of UFOs this would appear to be an understandable result of UFO activity, as interference with electronic power has been a consistent by-product of UFO presence in any vicinity.

In the Caribbean and in stock-raising areas in the United States, UFOs have been reported as having been seen where grazing or coralled animals have been found mysteriously slaughtered overnight and drained of blood, again attributing to UFO occupants a somewhat ghoulish but again understandable taste or need for blood, or perhaps even a desire to analyze it. Another unusual activity which has been attributed to UFOs is the stocking or scattering of unusual animals in different locations on Earth, the animals or creatures being noted after UFOs have been in the vicinity. These include reports of archaic forms of sea life and unidentified species of rays in the waters of the Triangle, anthropoid specimens like 'Big Foot' in forested parts of the Pacific Coast of the United States, Florida, and even New Jersey and Pennsylvania, puma-type giant cats in England, and other assorted monsters throughout the world, none of which logically should be there.

The killing of farm animals and draining of their blood, often with the removal, as if by near surgical excision, of parts of the animal, such as the eyes, tongue, muzzle, or genitals, may quite possibly be the work of either cultists or eccentrics wishing to keep a mystery going. The appearance of new or unfamiliar species of animals, however appealing the idea of them coming from another planet or dimension, must of course be discounted until they can be positively identified.

These and like incidents are basically indications of how UFOs are suspected in popular opinion of being connected with unusual incidents for which an easy explanation is lacking. They reflect a willingness on the part of sections of the public to believe that UFOs and the intelligences that guide them are not simply reconnoitering our planet but landing on it for a variety of reasons, some suspected but most of them undiscerned.

Another factor contributing to a theory that extraterrestrials are already among us is the 'Men in Black' concept, well known to all researchers of UFO phenomena and described in detail by theorists and writers over the years, such as John Keel, Albert Bender, Gray Barker, and Brad Steiger, to name but a few. The Men in Black might be described as a sort of extraterrestrial (or other) warning system directed against 'earthlings' who have seen UFOs. Numerous individuals who have sighted or been in contact with UFOs claim to have been visited shortly thereafter by a man, or three men, of olive complexion, dressed in black, and often using large black cars (Cadillacs!) as means of transportation. During these visits the persons who have just had UFO experiences are allegedly warned by the Men in Black not to discuss further what they have seen. Sometimes they are warned by telephone, often repeatedly, and sometimes they are warned even before they have told anyone else about their experiences.

If the Men in Black are not extraterrestrials trying to keep their visits secret, a second good guess would be that they have a more earthly origin – from government, local, or private agencies. They might have as their aim the minimizing of publicity or public excitement, the safeguarding of a local investigation of the subject, or even the protection of a secret experiment. Also, some of the warning telephone calls may come from erratic individuals for the purpose of causing additional excitement, especially in cases where UFO sightings have been reported in the local press. The Men in Black are not limited to the United States, but seem to be a world-wide phenomenon, according to reports reached through the curtain of local censorship.

Still, some of the unusual suicides or apparent murders of active researchers, two of them connected directly with the Bermuda Triangle, although possibly coincidental, are thought provoking. Dr James McDonald, an astrophysicist who was greatly involved with and preoccupied by the study of UFOs, apparently shot himself under mysterious circumstances, in the desert under the night skies of Arizona in 1971. Dr Morris Jessup, a brilliant astronomer and investigator and writer on UFOs, committed suicide in his car in a Miami park while on his way to deliver a manuscript, on which he had been working for some years, to Dr Manson Valentine. The report concerned the 'Philadelphia Experiment,' regarding the potentiality of the use of intensified magnetism to induce invisibility and teleportation as an explanation of what was happening in the Bermuda Triangle. (This case will be more fully discussed in the following chapter.) Chuck Wakeley, a young Miami pilot who, after almost losing his plane and his life in a luminous cloud in the Triangle, began seriously to study other Bermuda Triangle incidents and their attendant circumstances. He wrote about them, lectured, and appeared on TV and radio programs discussing the Bermuda Triangle. He was shot through a window of his ground-floor apartment in Miami in 1974 while working on his research – the assailant and motive are still unknown.

These are isolated incidents; the suicides of the space scientists were perhaps connected with the UFO question only through the depression generated in scientists by their rejection by the scientific establishment once they began to specialize in research too closely connected with UFOs. Considering that our physical and astro scientists, who have advanced theories during the past few years that encompass suppositions that our minds can barely grasp, such as antimatter, negatively charged matter existing in the universe which, on encountering positively charged matter, would cause a mutually destructive explosion; the black holes in space, thought to be the result of great nova star bursts falling in on themselves and causing a concentration of nuclei wherein the attraction would swallow other matter – planets, stars, or light itself, compacting them to so small a size that a speck of such matter could weigh more than our earth; the curvature of space through which theory the trajectory of travel to distant stars might take much less time than previously supposed; and the theory of the expanding universe, based on the Doppler effect, originally a sound phenomenon. One may therefore wonder why the scientific establishment persistently avoids theories involving the presence of thought coming from somewhere not of this earth. These extraterrestrial thought processes would be, of necessity, implied even to theorize about the activity and purpose of UFOs and their control of fields of operation from beyond Earth.

Popular enthusiasm and prescience often precede scientific acceptance or willingness to accept new concepts. Some astro-scientific circles, however, now appear willing to contemplate the near future with an open mind, as is indicated by the following extract from a report of the Astronomy Survey Committee of the United States National Academy of Sciences:

> Each passing year has seen our estimates of the probability of life in space increase, along with our capabilities for detecting it. More and more scientists feel that contact with other civilizations is no longer something beyond our dreams but a natural event in the history of mankind that will perhaps occur within the lifetime of many of us. The promise is now too great, either to turn away from it or to wait much longer before devoting major resources to a search for other intelligent beings ... In the long run this may be one of science's most important and most profound contributions to mankind and to our civilization.

One of the factors usually mentioned regarding the unlikelihood or impossibility of making direct contact with other advanced forms of life in the universe is that it would take more than a human life-span to reach another planetary system (supposing our own has no other inhabited planets) where life may have evolved. But if one could travel at the speed of light, a limit to the speed of material objects attributed to Einstein, then intergalactic travel would be possible within our own life-span, with certain odd modifications which flow from the relationship between the speed of a material object and time. For example, if we could travel to Alpha Centauri at the speed of light, a matter of three and a half clock years in a space capsule, and then return to Earth, we would be seven years older but we would find that twenty years had passed on Earth. This relativity of speed and time can be even more strikingly illustrated when we consider that, if it were possible to make a round trip to Andromeda, the nearest galaxy to our own, the voyage at the speed of light would take fifty-six clock years in the space capsule, although the astronauts would find on their return that the earth had aged two million years. These suppositions are bounded by limits on the speed of matter as well as to the distance to the far stars. But what if Einstein's theory of the curvature of space is correct and that a straight line projected into space would become a circle? What if matter itself could be disassociated and reprojected? Although such concepts appear illogical, we cannot possibly know at this point how advanced in scientific development older civilizations in the cosmos (always presuming that they exist) may be. It might explain not only the misty appearances and disappearances of UFOs over the waters of the Bermuda Triangle and elsewhere but also the disappearance and reappearance under certain conditions of intensified magnetism, of our air and surface craft and their occupants.

Again, if it is not a matter of outer space, perhaps our own craft have gone into and the strange craft have come out of another dimension – one of the worlds within worlds which may occupy our own universe at the same time as we are but only occasionally coinciding, either when conditions are haphazardly suitable or when they are brought purposely into what we may call 'crossover' contact.

In either case, the road to other worlds may be closer than we have previously imagined, if we can find it or if we wish to travel on it. Though we may already have taken the first step without knowing it – in 1943, almost as a by-product of a research experiment reportedly carried out by the United States Navy. Part of this alleged experiment happened in waters slightly to the north of the Bermuda Triangle.

CHAPTER TEN

ROADS TO OTHER WORLDS

In mid-October 1943, the United States Navy allegedly conducted a series of tests at the Philadelphia Navy Yard, at Norfolk-Newport News, Virginia, and at sea. Although a certain amount has been written about the 'Philadelphia Experiment' in books, magazines, and both domestic and foreign newspapers, basic sources of information remain clouded. Witnesses have died, other witnesses or informed personnel refuse to be quoted, and at least one researcher has committed suicide. Even its Navy code name is apparently unknown; if it were established, researchers would be able to consult the basic documents, if they still exist or are not too highly classified. Nevertheless, persistent reports and comment about the Philadelphia Experiment follow the same pattern: an attempt to make a Navy ship 'disappear' in a 1943 experiment was eminently successful, except for the deleterious effect on the crew.

The connection between the Philadelphia Experiment and the Bermuda Triangle stems from the reported use of an artifically induced magnetic field to cause the temporary disappearance of a destroyer and crew. Its advantage to naval warfare lies, of course, in the camouflage possibilities implied in rendering warships invisible. But its importance to scientific theory is more profound: men and matériel were temporarily projected into another dimension.

Dr Manson Valentine, a friend and colleague of Dr Morris Jessup, the prominent astronomer and selenographer who became involved with the Office of Naval Research after the experiment reportedly occurred, has outlined some of the more striking incidents of the Philadelphia Experiment as he remembers them through his conversations and correspondence with Dr Jessup.

According to Jessup the purpose [of the Philadelphia Experiment] was to test out the effect of a strong magnetic field on a manned surface craft. This was to be accomplished by means of magnetic generators (degaussers). Both pulsating and non-pulsating generators were operated to create a tremendous magnetic field on and around a docked vessel. The results were as astonishing as they were important, although with unfortunate aftereffects on the crew. When the experiment first began to take effect, a hazy green light became evident, something like reports we have from survivors of incidents in the Triangle who tell of a luminous greenish mist. Soon the whole ship was full of this green haze and the craft, together with its personnel, began disappearing from sight of those on the dock until only its water line was visible. The destroyer was subsequently reported to have appeared and disappeared at Norfolk, Virginia, which may have been the result of a trial invisibility run, involving a related time-warp phenomenon.

It was reported ... that the experiment was successful at sea with an effective invisibility of spheroid shape extending 100 yards from each beam, which showed the impression made by the ship in the water, but not the ship itself. As the force field intensified some crew members began disappearing and had to be rediscovered by tactual contact and restored to visibility by a sort of laying on of hands technique ... full recovery could by a serious problem. It was rumored that many were hospitalized, some died, others were adversely affected mentally.

Psychic ability seemed to have been generally sharpened, while many retained the effects of transmutation from the experiment, temporarily disappearing and reappearing, either at home, walking on the street, or sitting in bars or restaurants, to the consternation of onlookers and waitresses. Twice the ship's binnacle suddenly burst into flames while being taken ashore, with disastrous results to the carrier.

The connection between Jessup and the Philadelphia Experiment was fortuitous or destined, according to one's interpretation. Dr Jessup, who through his career as an astronomer had consistently inclined toward a study of UFOs, published an early book on the subject entitled *The Case for the UFO* – Citadel Press, New York, 1955. Sometime subsequent to publication he read, among what he first thought to be letters in the normal run of fan mail, a two-part handwritten communication from a person who signed himself Carl M. Allen (but Carlos Miguel Allende on the return address), containing references to a Navy experiment, at the Philadelphia Navy Yard and at sea, with names, dates, and rather unusual details. Consideration of some sections of this correspondence suggests why Jessup, as a scientist, found it so interesting that he replied with a request for more information. In the first letter, starting with a discussion of Einstein's 'unified field' theory, the writer stated:

The 'result' was complete invisibility of a ship, Destroyer type, *and all* of its crew, while at sea. (Oct. 1943) The field was effective in an oblate spheroidal shape, extending one hundred yards (more or less, due to lunar positions and latitude) *out* from each beam of the ship. Any person within that sphere became vague in form BUT he too observed those persons aboard *that* ship as though they too were of the same state, yet were walking upon nothing. Any person without that sphere should see nothing save the *clearly defined shape of the ship's hull in the water*, providing, of course, that the person was just close enough to see, yet just barely outside of that field. Why tell you now? Very simple; if you choose to go mad, then you would reveal this information. Half of the officers and the crew of that ship are at present mad as hatters. A few are even yet confined to certain areas where they may receive trained scientific aid when they either 'Go Blank' or 'Go Blank and Get Stuck'. Going Blank i.e., an after effect of the man having been within the field too much, is not at all an unpleasant experience to healthily curious sailors. However it is when also, they 'Get Stuck' that they call it 'HELL INCORPORATED'. The man thusly stricken cannot move of his own volition unless two or more of those who are within the field go and touch him, quickly, else he 'Freezes'.

If a man freezes, his position must be marked out carefully and then the field is cut off. Everyone but that 'frozen' man is able to move; to appreciate *apparent* solidarity again. Then, the newest member of the crew must approach the spot, where he will find the 'frozen' man's face or bare skin, that is not covered by usual uniform clothing. Sometimes, it takes only an hour or so, sometimes all night and all day long, and worse, it once took 6 months, to get a man 'unfrozen'.

... Deep 'frozen men' are not aware of time as we know it. They are like semi-comatose persons, who live, breathe, look and feel but still are unaware of so utterly many things as to constitute a 'Nether World' to them. A man in an ordinary common freeze *is* aware of time, sometimes *acutely* so. Yet they are never aware of time precisely as you or I are aware of it. The first 'Deep Freeze' as I said took 6 months to rectify. It also took over 5 million dollars worth of electronic equipment and a special ship berth. If, around or near the Philadephia Navy Yard you see a group of sailors in the act of putting their hands upon a fellow *or* upon 'thin air', observe the digits and appendages of the stricken man. If they seem to waver, as though within a heat mirage, *go quickly* and put your hands upon him, *for that man is the very most desperate of men in the world. Not one of those men ever want at all to become again invisible.* I do not think that much more need be said as to why man is not ready for force-field work.

You will hear phrases from these men such as 'caught in the Flow' (or the 'push') or 'Stuck in the Green' or 'Stuck in Molasses' or 'I was going fast', these refer to some of the decade-later after effects of force field work. 'Caught in the Flow' describes exactly the 'Stuck in Molasses' sensation of a man going into a 'deep freeze' or 'plain freeze' either of the two. 'Caught in the Push' can either refer to that which a man feels briefly when he is either about to inadvertently 'Go Blank' i.e., become invisible *or* about to 'Get Stuck' in a 'deep freeze' or 'plain freeze'.

There are only a very few of the original Experimental D-E's crew left by now ... Most went insane, one just

walked 'through' his quarters wall in sight of his wife and
child and two other crew members (was never seen again),
two 'went into the flame' i.e., they 'froze' and caught fire
while carrying common small-boat compasses, one man
carried the compass and caught fire, the other came for the
'laying on of hands' as he was nearest but he too, took
fire.... The faith in 'hand laying' died when this happened
and mens minds went by the score ...

... The experiment was a complete success. The men
were complete failures....

The balance of the original letter was concerned with
suggestions to Jessup of how the report could be checked
and other witnesses found. Jessup, his interest aroused, replied to the letter and asked for further proof of Allende's
allegations. Within several months 'Allen' wrote again this
time offering to take sodium pentothal and subject himself
to a hypnotist so that he could recall names and facts involved in the incident, which he, as an apparent witness,
considered so important. Allen thought, however, that the
Office of Naval Research would never 'let it be known that
any such thing was ever allowed to be done.' In this second
letter he added a theory of his own:

I feel that if handled properly, i.e., presented to people and
science in the proper psychologically effective manner, I feel
sure that man will go where he now dreams of being ... to
the stars through the form of transport that the Navy ac-
cidently stumbled upon (to their embarrassment) when their
experimental ship took off and popped up a minute or so
later on several hundred sea-travel-trips miles away at another of its berths in the Chesapeake Bay area ...

While Jessup was still considering the contents of the
second letter, he received an invitation from the Department of the Navy to come to the Office of Naval Research
(ONR) for an interview. When he presented himself at the
ONR Headquarters in Washington, D.C., he was, to his
considerable surprise, given a copy of his own book for ex-

amination. It was explained to him that the book had been
sent by mail to the Chief of ONR, Admiral F. N. Furth, in
the summer of 1955 and had been examined by officers in
the ONR Special Projects Office as well as the Aeronautics
Projects Office. The book was found to be filled with handwritten comments about Jessup's texts, apparently written
by three people who had passed or sent the book one to the
other and made their annotations in different colored inks.
When Jessup started to examine the book, he found that
the handwriting and style of one of the commentators was
evidently that of Allen, his mysterious correspondent. The
comments themselves were unusual for several reasons:
the commentators or critical reviewers of the text seemed
to assume the roles of representatives of a secret and ancient culture, having knowledge of previous scientific development on Earth and in the cosmos, constant visits to
Earth by interplanetary spacecraft and their means of travel
(as well as references to their method of operation), and
of an interplanetary war that had devasted Earth. The
comments were replete with references to force fields,
dematerialization, and the present observation of Earth by
great and small space ships. However, along with these
apparent science fictional fancies, these comments made
specific reference to secret naval experiments, especially
the Philadelphia Experiment of 1943. Thus Jessup found
himself again involved, through his book, in this curious
affair, and, according to what he told several of his colleagues, he began to investigate the subject through his
now established contact with the Navy. However, his unexpected and unexplained death in 1959 ended his research.

Meanwhile, a limited number of copies of Dr Jessup's
book, mimeographed along with the complete series of
puzzling annotations by the unidentified commentators,
had been reproduced, apparently at the request of the U.S.
Navy or of individual naval officers, by a Texas electronics
firm, the Varo Corporation of Dallas. Coincidentally this
company was performing special (or secret) work for the

Department of the Navy.

The reproduction of the annotated edition and subsequent dissemination within naval and military circles contains the germ of yet another mystery, for, if the information handwritten on the original copy of the book were incorrect or imaginary, why should a limited edition be circulated within the Pentagon? The original Jessup book, without annotations, had caused no special stir, and apparently only the annotations with their 'informed' references to naval experiments had provoked official interest.

Gray Barker, a writer and UFO researcher, who finally came into possession of one of these difficult-to-obtain annotated copies, remembers how he first heard about it:

> I first learned of the annotated copy when I was talking to Mrs Walton Colcord John, Director of the *Little Listening Post*, a UFO and New Age Publication in Washington. Speaking over the telephone Mrs John told me of a strange rumor going around, to the effect that somebody had sent a marked-up copy to Washington and that the government had gone to the expense of mimeographing the entire book, so that all the underlinings and notations could be added to the original text. This was being sent around rather widely, she told me, through military channels.
>
> She had not, of course, seen a copy of it, and didn't know too much about it, but somehow she seemed to connect it with an alleged Naval experiment wherein a ship had completely disappeared from sight. I couldn't make too much out of all this until later I had also heard about the strange Allende Letters, which told of such an experiment in a most horrifying way.

Despite the scarcity of the reproduced annotated edition, most of the copies having disappeared either by chance or perhaps by design, Gray Barker was able to preserve a copy and has since reproduced a small edition for sale to interested researchers (*The Case for the UFO – Annotated Edition*, Gray Barker, Clarksburg, West Virginia).

The apparent suicide of Dr Jessup deserves an additional

comment. During the time between his first call from the Navy and his death he devoted a good deal of research to the Philadelphia Experiment and, while carefully observing the lines of security regulations, shared with Dr Valentine some of his general findings and theories.

Jessup told Valentine that the Navy had tried to find Allende (or Allen) from the return address on his correspondence with Jessup but had been unable to do so and, of course, had no leads on the identity of the two other commentators. Jessup was convinced that the experiment had actually taken place and that the attendant incidents had occurred as described. He considered that the unfortunate results as far as personnel were concerned were probably due to insufficient preparation or screening. Several experiments had apparently taken place, some at pierside and a rather dramatic and perhaps inadvertent one at sea, when the destroyer disappeared from convoy duty and reappeared at its berth at Norfolk and then shifted back to its dock at the Philadelphia Navy Yard.

Jessup was worried about the experiments and told Valentine that the Navy had requested him to be a consultant on yet another experiment but that he had refused. He was convinced that the Navy, in seeking to create a magnetic cloud for camouflage purposes in October 1943, had uncovered a potential that could temporarily, and if strong enough perhaps permanently, rearrange the molecular structure of people and materials so that they would pass into another dimension with further implications of predictable and as yet uncontrolled teleportation. When Valentine, a student of the Bermuda Triangle mystery since 1945, suggested that what was happening within the Triangle was a result of the same phenomenon on a larger scale, Jessup tentatively agreed.

Toward the middle of April 1959, Jessup told Valentine that he had reached what he considered to be some definite conclusions about the series of reactions implied by the Philadelphia Experiment and had prepared a rough draft that he wished to discuss. Dr Valentine suggested that he come to dinner. The invitation was for the evening of April 20.

He never came to dinner. At some time before 6:30 P.M., Jessup, according to police reports, drove his car to Matheson's Hammock, a Dade County park in the Miami area, and apparently committed suicide by carbon monoxide inhalation, after attaching a hose to the exhaust and running the hose inside his car. No notes or manuscript was mentioned in the police report, nor, according to a statement by a witness later given to Dr Valentine, were any found inside the car.

Dr Valentine has mentioned an aspect of the incident also not covered in the official report – that Dr Jessup was still alive when first found, adding: '... perhaps he was allowed to die. His theories were very advanced and perhaps there were ... influences that wished to prevent their spreading ...'

The more one digs into this alleged experiment the more curious it becomes. Certain elements of information can be verified but none referring directly to the experiment. A number of persons in and out of the Navy profess to remember the incident and are even willing to furnish more information about it, except that they are unwilling to be quoted by name. The circumstances are often considerably embellished: Navy Yard personnel seem to remember stories and even short newspaper articles about a sailors' brawl in a Philadelphia bar where some of the participants vanished and reappeared out of a haze during the fight, to the surprise and discomfort of their opponents. The approximate date of the main incident is generally agreed on and the consensus among people employed at the docks at the time was that something very unusual was going on at the Philadelphia Navy Yard.

Whatever the truth of the incident, the destroyer mentioned as taking part in the experiment, the U.S.S. *Eldridge*, D-173, *did* exist. It was commissioned August 27, 1943, and was engaged in escort and patrol missions around Bermuda, Chesapeake Bay, and the seas between until early

1944, when it was sent across the Atlantic and could therefore fit within the time frame indicated. The ship was decommissioned in June 1946 and eventually transferred, under the Mutual Defense Assistance Program, to Greece, where, one might hope, it ceased to display its attributed propensity for disappearing. The Liberty ship S.S. *Andrew Furuseth*, from the decks of which the disappearance of the D-173 was allegedly seen, was also actually in the area at the time indicated, as was the S.S. *Malay*, another cargo ship that reportedly witnessed the same or subsequent incidents.

Efforts to contact or interrogate some of the presumed participants or observers of the incident have generally proved unsuccessful, as many have disappeared, others have proved uncommunicative, and others reply that they do not wish to get involved or are protected by family members who relay the message that they do not wish to talk about it.

If a confidential or secret freeze has really been established over the Navy or merchant ships and personnel involved directly or indirectly in the experiment at the time, then the verification of the incident would be extremely difficult to follow through, especially since it occurred so long ago. It should be observed in passing, however, that the full import of an experiment is often not realized or apparent until years after the initial tests.

It may also be possible that personnel who were involved with other camouflage incidents during World War II may have given rise to a series of rumors that contributed to the Philadelphia Experiment legend. Dunninger, the famous clairvoyant and telepath, approached the U.S. Navy in 1942 with a plan for making a Navy ship invisible through a process of mirages induced by manipulation of the sun's rays. (Whatever the result of his activity, he was obliged to sign a paper guaranteeing his complete and permanent silence regarding the operation.) Several other unusual concepts, including the military use of antigravity, were also a subject of experimentation.

An investigator working with the Navy and possessed of a knowledge of Navy filing practices as well as a strong desire for anonymity confided to the author that he had tried for months at the Pentagon and elsewhere to locate ONR reports dealing with the original experiment but had been unsuccessful. 'However,' he added, 'I did find one unusual thing. The framework is set up and the experiment is still continuing.'

Although Jessup's final conclusions may never be known, some of the ideas exchanged by Drs Jessup and Valentine during their discussions of the Philadelphia Experiment and its relation to the Bermuda Triangle are echoed in the following answers by Dr Valentine to some questions put to him by the author:

Question: *You have previously said that Dr Jessup thought that the U.S. Navy had inadvertently discovered the natural or induced combination of circumstances that caused the disappearances in the Triangle. Could you comment on this more fully?*

I do not believe Dr Jessop considered this an 'inadvertent' discovery. For many years, so I have been told, experiments involving high intensity magnetism have been officially discouraged, just as the ion motors, known for as far back at least as 1918, have been denied public disclosure and their inventors somehow silenced. I therefore am convinced that top ranking physicists must have some knowledge – and understandable dread – of phenomena that might be expected to emerge from the generation of a high intensity magnetic field, especially a pulsating or vortexual one.

In the case of the alleged Philadelphia Experiment is there a fairly simple scientific explanation as to what took place?

To my knowledge there is no explanation in terms of the familiar or orthodox. Many scientists now share the opinion that basic atomic structure is essentially electric in nature rather than materially particulate. A vastly complicated interplay of energies is involved. Such a broad concept lends great flexibility to the universe. If multiple phases of matter within such a cosmos did *not* exist, it would be most surprising.

The transition from one phase to another would be equivalent to the passage from one plane of existence to another – a sort of interdimensional metamorphosis. In other words, there could be 'worlds within worlds.' Magnetism has long been suspect as an involvement agent in such potentially drastic changes. To begin with, it happens to be the only inanimate phenomenon for which we have been unable to conceive a mechanistic analogue. We can visualize electrons traveling along a conductor and thus 'explain' electric current, or we can envisage energy waves of different frequencies in the ether and thus 'explain' the heat-light-radio spectrum. But a magnetic field defies a mechanical interpretation. There is something almost mystical about it. Furthermore, whenever we encounter incredible (to us) materialization and dematerialization, as in UFO phenomena, they seem to be accompanied by severe magnetic disturbances. It is, therefore, reasonable to suppose that a purposeful genesis of unusual magnetic conditions could effect a change of phase in matter, both physical and vital. If so, it would also distort the time element which is by no means an independent entity, but part-in-parcel of a particular matter – energy-time dimension such as the one we live in.

If this is the result of intensification of magnetism, are there, in your opinion, intensified magnetic fields sporadically active or 'on the loose' in the Triangle?

I believe that this is unquestionably the case. Either the magnetic fields are the result of sporadic, perhaps seasonal buildup of geophysical origin, or they are the concomitant effects of UFO activity. Possibly a combination of both agencies can occur. Another important aspect to consider is the likelihood of magnetic, cyclonic storms initiated by either condition. Like the tornado, the magnetic vortex would be self-augmenting and could well bring about an interdimensional transition for anyone caught up in it. The experience of Bruce Gernon is a case in point. [See Chapter 7.]

Do you have an opinion as to whether these fields are natural or induced?

It is my opinion that the buildup of magnetic force fields in the Triangle may be due to a combination of natural causes and induction by UFO activity. 'Space engineers' may be utilizing the electrical potential of a very special area of the earth, at the same time creating severe magnetic storms when they move. As I have stated before, these interdimensional craft may be quite invisible to us while their presence in our atmosphere is being felt magnetically. Radar, however, may pick them up, at least temporarily.

As a veteran observer of the disappearances in the Bermuda Triangle, do you think that an acceptable explanation will be found in the near future?

I believe an acceptable explanation of interdimensional phenomena must await a more universal recognition of the objectivity of these phenomena than we are officially willing to concede today. It will happen only when existing 'explanatory' theories give way to a better understanding of natural principles. We arrive at the latter by correlating uncensored data – I mean *all* available data regardless of whether or not such data support preconceived theory. We must raise our scientific sights from the old obstructionist, deductive method (letting the facts fit the theory) to the more intelligent inductive method (letting the facts shape a principle). At the rate this involvement now seems to be progressing among our younger scientists, a state of enlightenment for many of us could well be within our grasp in the very near future.

Whether the Philadelphia Experiment actually took place or not is difficult to prove. The concept, however, is a valid one, having been perhaps suggested or supported by Einstein's 'unified field' theory, an attempt logically to bring together the magnetic and gravitational fields and other subatomic phenomena. In application both to the Philadelphia Experiment and to the Bermuda Triangle, the attraction between molecules could be temporarily altered by a force field. It would, in effect, introduce matter into another dimension or, one might say, the etheric world. Such force fields comprise both the cause and effect of the transmutation and transference of matter. If this seems impossible or illogical, one might reflect that another seemingly impossible theory of Einstein and others has modified our lives and physical outlook since 1945 to the point where those of us who lived before that time would hardly recognize our former personalities, so secure in our dominion of the earth and understanding of our section of the universe.

It is a truism to say that humanity stands on the brink of a plunge into the cosmos, having already made certain tentative steps and then hesitating while the exigencies for the further development of destructive warfare make their demands upon the budgets of the earth's nations. Exploration of the far reaches of this galaxy and others may await the development of new concepts concerning the possibility of projecting matter into other dimensions and across the void between the stars.

Columbus, as he pondered his projected voyage from the docks of various Atlantic ports, faced somewhat similar problems; the takeoff into the unknown as well as the means of funding his exploration. Tentative steps had already been taken by others in the exploration of the Ocean Sea, such as the discovery of the Canary Islands, Madeira, and the Azores, corresponding for the purposes of this comparison to our own already accomplished voyages to the moon and probes of the planets.

As Columbus pursued his researches in various ports along the Atlantic littoral, he noted an unusual occurrence that took place in Galway, Ireland, when a strange longboat washed up on the Irish shore containing two corpses, clad in skins, whom the local inhabitants, naturally unfamiliar with Eskimos or American Indians, considered to be Chinese.

There was considerable conjecture about how the weird-looking corpses had come to Galway in their strange boat. Columbus, however, instinctively realized that, whoever they were, they had come from the other side of the ocean, and this odd preview of a west-to-east voyage fortified him in his theories and resolve.

Perhaps the Bermuda Triangle, another, greater mystery of the Atlantic, is at the same time an indication and a beacon to stranger and even further voyages. Perhaps it is *already* serving others as a road, while for us, when we learn how to control the principles involved, it may prove to be the gateway to our own road to the stars and to the multiple worlds of the galaxies which surround us.

Remembering Columbus, standing on the brink of the discovery of the New World, one may observe, however we feel about the justice of the European incursion, that it subsequently proved unquestionably better for survival purposes, to have been a questing and curious European rather than a nonquesting Amerindian, the greater number of which were destined for extinction. It is likely that intelligent entities are questing in outer and inner space. It will be better for us to continue to explore and search on our own, preferably as a united planet, rather than passively to await discovery and settlement of *our* world by other travelers on the road to and from the stars.

Acknowledgments

The author wishes to express his appreciation to the following persons and organizations who have contributed advice, suggestions, expertise, information, drawings, or photographs to this book. Mention in this regard of any individual or organization does not, of course, imply their acceptance or knowledge of or agreement with any of the theories expressed in this book except those specifically attributed to them.

The author wishes to express his special appreciation to J. Manson Valentine, Ph.D., curator honoris of the Museum of Science of Miami and research associate of the Bishop Museum of Honolulu, for his drawings, maps, photographs, and interviews, as quoted in the text.

The following names are listed in alphabetical order:
Isaac Asimov, scientist, author, lecturer.
Gray Barker, author, publisher.
Bahama Air Sea Rescue Association.
Lin Berlitz, diver, researcher.
Valerie Berlitz, author, artist.
Carolyn Blakemore, editor.
Bob Brush, pilot, diver, photographer.
Hugh Lynn Cayce, president, Association for Research and Enlightenment.
Ray Clarke, equipment supervisor, passenger liners.
Cynthia Coffey, writer, researcher.
Gene Condon, captain, private submarine *Margenaut*.
Hadley Doty, merchant marine investigator.
Julius Egloff, Jr, oceanographer.

Barry Farber, radio commentator.
Reverend Salvador Freixedo, author, lecturer.
Vincent Gaddis, author.
Bruce Gernon, pilot.
John Godwin, author.
Carlos González, UFO researcher.
Grenada Tourist Office.
Captain Don Henry, shipmaster, diver, salvor.
Ben Huggard, long-distance swimmer, police officer.
Dr J. Allen Hynek, astronomer, author, UFO researcher.
Emily Ingram, court reporter.
Theodora Kane, educator, artist.
John Keel, author, UFO researcher.
Robert Kuhne, engineer.
Edward E. Kuhnel, attorney: specialist, oceanic law.
The Library of Congress.
Lloyd's of London.
Captain Gene Lore, senior pilot, TWA.
Margen International, underwater exploration.
Captain Marvin McCamis, yacht builder, captain private
    submarine.
Dr Robert J. Menzies, oceanographer, author.
Jacques Mayol, diver, author.
Professor Wayne Meshejian, physicist.
Howard Metz, UFO researcher.
William Morris, lexicographer, author, columnist.
Gordon T. Morris, writer, columnist.
Bruce Mounier, professional fisherman, diver.
National Aeronautics and Space Administration.
Jerry Osborn, former antisubmarine warfare technician,
    U.S.N.
Dimitri Rebikoff, oceanographer, inventor, diver, author.
Robert P. Reilly, former petty officer, U.S.N.
Jim Richardson, pilot, diver.
John Sander, writer, lecturer, radio commentator.
Seaman's Institute Library.
Captain Raymond Shattenkirk, pilot (retired), Pan Am.
Society for the Investigation of the Unexplained.

Gardener Soule, oceanographer, author.

Gene Steinberg, writer, lecturer, radio commentator.

Joe Talley, shark fisherman.

Jim Thorne, oceanographer, author, publisher, photographer, diver.

United States Air Force.

United States Coast Guard.

United States Navy.

Maxime B. Vollmer, mythologist, philologist.

Robert Waddington, school director.

Robert Warth, research chemist.

West of England Shipowners Mutual Protection and Indemnity Association.

Richard Winer, author, diver, film maker.

Roy H. Wirshing, Lieutenant Commander, U.S.N., Retired, author, lecturer.

Dr David D. Zink, university professor, archaeologist.

Bibliography

Bailey, Maurice and Marilyn, *Staying Alive*. New York, 1974.

Baker, Ralph, *Great mysteries of the Air*. Chatto, London, 1966.

Baxter, John, and Atkins, Thomas, *The Fire Came By*. New York, 1976.

Bender, Albert K., *Flying Saucers and the Three Men*. New York, 1962.

Berlitz, Charles, *The Mystery of Atlantis*. Souvenir Press, London, 1976.

——, *Mysteries from Forgotten Worlds*. Souvenir Press, London, 1972.

——, *The Bermuda Triangle*. Souviner Press, London, 1975.

Blake, George, *Lloyd's Register of Shipping, 1760–1960*. Crawley, Sussex, England, 1960.

Busson, Bernard, and Leroy, Gerard, *The Last Secrets of Earth*. New York, 1956.

Byrd, Richard E., *Alone*. New York, 1938.

Cathie, B. L., and Temm, P. N., *Harmonic 695*. Christchurch, New Zealand, 1971.

Chatelain, Maurice, *Nos ancêtres venus du cosmos*. Paris, 1975.

Chevalier, Raymond, *L'Avion à la découverte du passé*. Paris, 1964.

Corliss, William R., *Mysteries Beneath the Sea*, New York, 1975.

Ebon, Martin (Ed.), *The Riddle of the Bermuda Triangle*. New York, 1972.

Freixedo, Salvador, *El Diabólico inconsciente*, Mexico, D. F., 1975.

Gaddis, Vincent, *Invisible Horizons*. Ace Books, London, 1975.

Godwin, John, *This Baffling World*. New York, 1968.

Hoyt, Edwin, *The Last Explorer*. New York, 1968.

Hynek, J. Allen, *The UFO Experience*. Abelard-Schuman, London & New York, 1972.

Jessup, M. K., *The Case for the UFO*. Annotated Edition, Clarksburg, West Virginia, 1973.

Keel, John A., *The Eighth Tower*. New York, 1975

——, *The Mothman Prophecies*. New York, 1975.

Keyhoe, Major Donald E., *Aliens from Space*. Panther, London, 1975.

Liedke, Klaus, and Szwitalski, Horst, *Die Meutreie auf der Mimi*, (Stern Magazin). Hamburg, 1975.

Muck, Otto, H., *Atlantis – Gefunden*. Stuttgart, 1954.

Robertson, Douglas, *Survive the Savage Sea*. Elek, London, 1973.

Sagan, Carl, *Intelligent Life in the Universe*. San Francisco, 1966.

Sanderson, Ivan T., *Invisible Residents*. Tandem, London, 1974.

Soule, Gardner, *Undersea Frontiers*. Chicago, 1968.

——, *Under the Sea*. New York, 1971.

——, *Men Who Dared the Sea*. New York, 1976.

Spencer, John Wallace, *Limbo of the Lost – Today*. Westfield, Massachusetts, 1975.

Steiger, Brad, and White, John, *Other Worlds – Other Universes*. New York, 1975.

Sullivan, Walter, *Continents in Motion*. McGraw Hill, London and New York, 1974.

Taylor, John G., *Black Holes*. Souvenir Press, London, 1973.

Vallée, Jacques, *Passport to Magonia*. Chicago, 1969.

Vallée, Jacques and Janine, *Challenge to Science*. Spearman, London, 1967.

Vignati, Alejandro, *El Triángulo mortal de las Bermudas*. Barcelona, 1975.

Villiers, Alan, *Posted Missing*. Hodder & Stoughton, London, 1975.

Wilkins, Harold T., *Strange Mysteries from Time and Space*. New York, 1959.

Winer, Richard, *The Devil's Triangle 2*. Corgi, London, 1976.

News Publications :

   BASRA's Compass   1975 and 1976

   Miami *Herald*   (since 1945)

   National Enquirer   1975 and 1976

   New York *Times*   1975 and 1976

   Saga   1975 and 1976

Also a variety of regional newspapers in the United States, and the British Commonwealth dealing with the disappearance of local residents within the Bermuda Triangle.

Fascinating Non-fiction Reading in Panther Books